MEDITATION FOR BEGINNERS

The Easiest Guide to Cultivate Awareness,
Acceptance, and Peace to Unleash
Your Inner Strength and Explore the
Deepest Realm of Your Being!!

Rohit Sahu

CONTENTS

AUTHOR NOTE

Dear Reader,

With great excitement and appreciation, I offer to you this book, the culmination of my spiritual studies. It's been a labor of love, knitted together to impart timeless knowledge and practical insights to improve your well-being and spiritual journey. I urge you to go on a transforming journey as you read through the pages of this book. Explore simple tactics, powerful rituals, and deep knowledge that you may incorporate into your everyday life.

Your thoughts and opinions are really valuable to me. I would be grateful if you could take a few seconds to leave a review on Amazon and share your ideas and experiences. Your review will not only help other readers make an informed decision, but it will also give vital insight into how this book has touched your life.

I sincerely ask you to share your thoughts, observations, and any recommendations you may have. Your thoughts will not only encourage me but will also help to evolve and refine the information and wisdom contained inside these pages.

May this book serve as a beacon of light for you in your spiritual journey.

With the deepest gratitude,

Rohit Sahu

FOREWORD

Meditation is an old tradition, yet it is still practiced in cultures all over the globe to promote inner peace and harmony. Although meditation has roots in many religious beliefs, it is more about expanding consciousness, gaining awareness, and experiencing peace than it is about religion.

It is a simple practice open to anyone, which may relieve stress, boost peace and clarity, and promote happiness. Learning how to meditate is simple, and the benefits can come shortly.

Meditation has been practiced for thousands of years. Meditation initially was designed to aid enhance knowledge of the sacred and mystical aspects of existence. These days, meditation is extensively used for relaxation and stress reduction, as there is a growing need to decrease stress in our hectic schedules and demanding life. It is considered a sort of mind-body alternative therapy. Meditation can promote a profound level of relaxation and a peaceful mind.

During meditation, you try to remain aware and surf the stream of muddled thoughts and emotions. This process may result in better physical and emotional well-being.

Meditation started in India and evolved with Hinduism (Sanatana Dharma) and Yoga. Some of the oldest references to meditation are found in Rig Veda, around 5000 BCE, in India. In the 5th and 6th century BCE meditation was founded in Buddhism and Jainism, followed by the Islamic Sufi order. References to meditation are also found in the Torah of Judaism. In Christianity, meditation is used to signify a kind of prayer where the faithful focus upon the revelations of God. Today meditation is practiced all across the globe without any connection to religious context, yet the methods remain as they were thousands of years ago.

In Hinduism, the fundamental purpose of meditation is to achieve oneness with one's soul (Atman) and connect with Brahman, the omnipresent and all-powerful god, with the ultimate aim being to achieve Moksha (Nirvana in Buddhism). Certain postures—yoga—are outlined in Hindu texts to achieve a meditative state. Yoga and meditation are mentioned multiple times in ancient Indian writings, such as the Vedas, Upanishads, Mahabharata, and the Bhagavad Gita. Meditation is defined by the Brihadaranyaka Upanishad as "being quiet and aware, one discovers the self (Atman) inside oneself."

The goal of meditation is to become consciously aware of or explore one's mind and body to get to know oneself. It is fundamentally both an exclusive and inclusive process in which one becomes an observer to every thought and distraction of the world and remains mindful of everything.

We may overcome mental obstacles, negative thinking, crippling worries, tension, and anxiety with the aid of meditation by understanding and dealing with the underlying causes. We gain insightful awareness in Dhyana, allowing us to manage our responses and reactions.

We learn the nature of the universe, the impermanence of our bodily existence, the fluctuations of our thoughts, the cause of our suffering, and how to resolve it through regular practice.

So, whether you want to ease stress, attain spiritual enlightenment, seek peace, or flow through movement, meditation is the way to go.

But how will we know which meditation practice is best for us as there are plenty of them?? While there are various types of meditation, each takes you to the same spot. It's like there are various routes to the same destination. So, it didn't matter which route you take. Here in this book, I'll discuss a certain type of meditation that is the easiest, most effective, and appreciated by most renounced yogis.

Although there is no right or incorrect method to meditate, it is important to select a practice that matches your requirements and compliments your nature. And the type of meditation I'm going to discuss here is ideal for anyone—from beginners to advanced.

The practice will inject far-reaching and long-lasting benefits into your life—lower stress, fewer struggles, better ability to connect, enhanced awareness, and being nicer to yourself are just some of its benefits. In this book, I'll lead you through the fundamentals of meditation, as well as its benefits, typical mistakes, misconceptions, FAQs, and various mudras and sitting postures. I'll also discuss the optimal environment, the right attitude, my own experience, and some pointers to help you grow.

So, if you're ready, let's embark on this quest beyond yourself...

INTRODUCTION TO MEDITATION

History

Meditation seems to be a simple concept—sit still, breathe normally, and observe. However, the practice of meditation has a long cultural history that has seen it evolve from a religious concept to something that might today seem more alluring than spiritual.

Meditation is a centuries-old technique that is said to have started in India thousands of years ago. Throughout history, the practice was gradually adopted by neighboring nations and became a part of numerous religions throughout the globe.

Around 1500 BCE, the first known writings that addressed meditation concerned Vedantism, a Hindu tradition in India. However, historians believe that meditation was practiced before this period, maybe as early as 3000 BCE.

Other meditation techniques were developed in Taoist China and Buddhist India between 600 and 500 BCE, however, the actual origins of these practices, notably Buddhist meditation, are still debated among historians. Meditation was seen to be a key component in the formula for moral salvation, contemplative focus, knowledge, and liberation.

Patanjali's Yoga Sutras, which outline the eight limbs of yoga, were composed between 400 and 100 BCE. The Bhagavad Gita, which describes the concept of yoga, meditation, and the discipline of living a spiritual life, was also composed during this period.

Although meditation and mindfulness practices are now used to achieve mental peace and other health benefits, meditation was originally a practice for religious people and wandering ascetics who sought to transcend the limitations of human life, connect with universal forces (personified as deities), and union with the transcendental reality through it (called Brahman in the Vedas).

The Hindu heritage of meditation includes both cave-meditating Yogis and Vedic culture's Sages (Rishis). It is the world's oldest meditation tradition, and it is still alive and well. It contains hundreds of methods and lineages. Mantra meditation or gazing was most likely the earliest meditation technique invented/ discovered; however, we don't know for sure.

The Technique's Significance

Meditation, according to modern science, is a technique in which a person directs his or her mind and creates a state of awareness to gain some advantage or for the mind to simply observe its contents without being involved with the content, or just as an end in itself. Within this wide concept, meditation is practiced in a variety of approaches with varying goals for the practitioners.

Some people use it to relax their minds, while others use it to promote positive thoughts in their minds, and yet others use it to improve their mind-power. Meditation is also said to have the ability to treat some ailments in the practitioner.

From the spiritual point of view, meditation is the practice of witnessing the inward and outward movement of thoughts as they enter and exit the mind with silence (Maunam), steadiness (Dhiram), and detachment (Vairagyam). It cleanses the mind of varied impressions formed as a result of action and reaction. Self-realization may occur in a pure state of mind via self-inquiry, which is the purpose of life in Hinduism, thus the significance of meditation. During meditation, one becomes a neutral observer of all thoughts as they come and go, and the mind eventually goes quiet. It isn't an experience since, in this state, the experiencer and the experience merge into one, and there is just oneness.

"Dhyana" is the Sanskrit term for meditation in Hinduism. "Dhi" means "receptacle" or "mind," and "Yana" means "movement" or "going." Dhyana is a Sanskrit word that signifies "journey" or "movement of the mind." It is a kind of mental activity (Dhi).

The mind (Manas) is considered in Hindu philosophy as a receptacle (Dhi) into which thoughts flow back and forth from the universal pool of thought-forms. According to the Hindu faith, the human intellect has God's creative potential. What you think about becomes who you are. You are the sum total of your thoughts and aspirations from this life as well as previous ones. What you think and want takes hold of you, becomes part of your latent imprints (Samskaras), and influences the trajectory of your life now and in the future.

These samskaras, which follow you to the next realm, decide the future trajectory of your existence. All of your mental activities, just like any physical activity, contribute to your Karma. Animals, too, have the power to grow into higher beings via mental effort.

We obtain insightful awareness in Dhyana or meditation, which allows us to manage our responses and reactions. We learn the nature of things, the impermanence of our bodily existence, the fluctuations of our thoughts, the cause of our suffering, and how to resolve it through regular practice. The distinction between meditation and contemplation is primarily intellectual in nature. As per some people, meditation is an enlightened observation, while contemplation is a focused reflection, with detachment being the common feature between the two.

According to Hindu creation theories, all creatures and universes emerged from God (referred to as Brahma in some texts and Brahman in others) solely through meditation. Its secrets and dimensions can only be grasped in transcendental moments of self-absorption, which are only achievable via meditation. Because each human is a carbon copy of the cosmos, we may comprehend the manifest world by understanding ourselves.

As a result, our ancient rishis used meditation and contemplation to uncover truths about themselves and the world around them. They saw the Vedic knowledge and the Universal Self in their profound meditating states. Since the information flowed out from the global awareness into their receptive and stable brains on its own, with no egoistic aim or selfishness, it is deemed not man-made (Apaurusheya), but divine and pure (Pramana).

MEDITATION BENEFITS

Meditation is becoming increasingly popular as more people become aware of its many health advantages. It is something that anyone can do to promote a feeling of calmness, tranquility, and balance, which may enhance your mental well-being, general health, and spiritual growth. It is convenient and easy, and no special equipment is required.

And the rewards don't cease when you finish meditating. Meditation may help you go through your day more peacefully and may help you manage symptoms of some medical illnesses. People also use it to cultivate other beneficial habits and feelings, such as a happy mindset and attitude, self-discipline, good sleep patterns, and even enhanced pain tolerance.

Below are 51 benefits of meditation that will inspire you to start meditating:

1. Meditation Helps Discover Your Purpose in Life

With the stress and fast speed of life in this modern era, many individuals question what their existence is all about. Have you ever considered the following questions: who am I, why am I here, what is my life's purpose, and what will bring me fulfilment?

Sitting in solitude in meditation is one way people reflect on these concerns. Spending time in meditation provides several possibilities to assist us to discover answers to such questions.

2. Morning Meditation is More Potent than Coffee

The explanation for this is that early morning meditators feel invigorated for the whole day without depending entirely on coffee. Starting the day with a 20-minute meditation practice stimulates the parasympathetic nervous system and produces energy-boosting endorphins, that wake us up and keep us more enthusiastic and fresher throughout the day.

3. Morning Meditation Activates Our Mental Filter

At any given moment, we are bombarded with thousands of stimuli. When the 'monkey mind' is active, we may get overwhelmed by the number of items fighting for our attention. Meditation, particularly in the morning, when the mind is clear of distractions and fresh after a good night's sleep, activates the mental spam filter.

As a result, we can remain more focused and aware throughout the day, and we can do tasks more efficiently. Morning meditation creates an overall state of peace in the mind and a general sense of well-being that lasts throughout the day.

4. It Enhances Empathy

Meditation activates neuronal connections in the brain that govern good emotions, such as empathy and compassion. Meditation generates a profound state of flow, which increases social connectivity and makes us more loving and friendly as individuals.

5. Promotes Emotional Health

Some types of meditation may help you have a better self-image and a more optimistic view of life.

For example, one study of almost 3,500 people showed that

meditation alleviated symptoms of depression.

Similarly, a meta-analysis of 18 trials found that patients undergoing meditation therapy had fewer depressive symptoms than those in a control group.

Another research discovered that those who conducted a meditation exercise had fewer negative thoughts in reaction to seeing negative pictures than those who did not.

Furthermore, inflammatory compounds known as cytokines, which are generated in reaction to stress, might have an impact on mood, leading to depression. According to a review of multiple researches, meditation may help ease depression by lowering levels of these inflammatory chemicals.

6. Decreases Inflammatory Disorders

Research done at the UW-Madison Waisman Centre in France and Spain found that practicing meditation had a variety of genetic and biochemical effects on individuals. Reduced levels of pro-inflammatory genes were shown to be associated with quicker physical recovery from a difficult situation.

Also, a group that undertook meditation training had better results at preventing cellular level inflammation than the control groups.

7. Improves Cognition Ability

Researchers believe that incorporating meditation into one's daily routine is a fantastic approach for professionals to boost their chances of success. According to research, both transcendent and mindful meditation practices increase the brain's problem-solving and decision-making skills, which may result in a positive change in our professional lives.

8. It Grows Your Wisdom by Deepening

Your Understanding

With just a few clicks, we may now access a multitude of information from all sectors of knowledge. But, even with all this information, are there any questions that you can't seem to find answers to?

There is a real treasure inside you that cannot be found by an online search. It is waiting for you deep inside. Instead of logging into a computer, you can use meditation to log into your own inner essence or soul. This will bring you to a wellspring of knowledge that will blossom your life.

9. Meditation is a Natural Stress Buster

One of the most popular reasons people practice meditation is to relieve stress. Stress is the body's reaction to unexpected adversity. In most cases, mental and physical stress raises levels of the stress hormone cortisol. Many of the negative consequences of stress are produced, such as the production of inflammatory molecules known as cytokines. These side effects may interfere with sleep, cause depression and anxiety, raise blood pressure, and lead to exhaustion and foggy thinking.

Facing immediate threats also raise the amount of cortisol, or stress hormone, in the body and activates the Autonomic Nervous system, which is in charge of fight-or-flight reactions.

Meditation is a direct line of defence against stress and burnout. It stimulates the pituitary gland in the brain, which causes endorphins, or happy hormones, to be released. It eventually dispels lethargy and re-energizes the reservoir of joy, creativity, and peacefulness.

Regular meditators have lower cortisol levels in their brains, which explains their resilience and inquisitive nature, according to brain research. They discovered that participants who began their workday with a brief meditation session felt more in touch with themselves and were able to cope with stress more readily.

Meditation has also been found in studies to reduce symptoms of stress-related diseases such as irritable bowel syndrome, post-traumatic stress disorder, and fibromyalgia.

10. It Increases Focus and Concentration Power

Meditation is similar to weight lifting for your attention span. It improves your attention's strength and endurance. Have you ever noticed how meditation draws you into the present moment? When we meditate, we naturally develop mindful awareness, and we achieve a state of 'flow,' in which our mind is in total harmony with itself.

Even those who meditate for a short period of time had greater attention than those who did not meditate at all.

Some research on meditation and its effects on attention found that it improves attention through modulating alpha brain waves. The brain's alpha waves control how we employ our sense organs and react to external stimuli.

Given the multitude of distractions in today's media-driven environment, the researchers devised an eight-week mindful meditation program, and tests found that individuals who finished the retreat had increased sensitivity to visual, aural, and tactile stimuli.

The brains of 17 participants were evaluated before and after they participated in an eight-week meditation program, according to the researchers. Gray matter increased in the areas of the brain important for learning, memory, and emotional control, according to brain scans.

Furthermore, a 2016 study conducted by Carnegie Mellon University researchers proved how mindfulness meditation might increase focus and decision-making.

11. It Promotes Better Fitness

Workouts and physical activity may not be enough to achieve peak fitness. Many scientists, nutritionists, and allied health science experts have highlighted that the key to fitness rests in a balanced lifestyle change that includes a healthy diet, physical activity, yoga, and meditation regularly.

Psychologists believe that the core objective of fitness is to ensure that the mind and body work in tandem. If our brains are filled with negative and anxious thoughts, we have very little chance of benefiting from any training regimen.

Meditation aids in the removal of limiting thoughts and self-beliefs, as well as giving a steady flow of motivation to the brain and body to keep going forward.

12. Results in Better Immunity

According to studies on the influence of meditation on cancer risk reduction, mindful relaxation and meditation techniques boost the body's lymphocyte count and aid in the development of a natural shield for battling harmful cells that cause the deadly illness.

Despite criticism, the study's results gave important data on how meditation might make us more resistant to painful diseases and illness.

13. Reduces Chance of Age-Related Memory Loss

Meditation, in addition to lowering stress, may help with age-related memory decline and memory retention issues. According to researchers, encouraging older persons to meditate for as little as two minutes each day may make a major impact on how they combat and manage memory dysfunctions.

It enhances performance in patients with age-related memory loss, according to studies.

Furthermore, early research suggests that diverse meditation methods may improve attention, memory, and mental sharpness in older participants, according to an analysis.

14. Provides Better Prognosis for Addiction

Overcoming substance abuse at any age needs a significant amount of self-control and discipline. Meditation may help break down the barrier of dry dependence. Meditation has been shown to change the brain receptors linked with drug and alcohol addiction, potentially reducing cravings for these drugs. Furthermore, meditation may heighten your awareness of cravings and help you better regulate them.

Meditation may help you establish mental discipline, which may help you overcome dependencies by boosting self-control and awareness of triggers for addictive behaviors.

A 2018 research published in Drug Abuse and Rehabilitation discovered that mindfulness training may assist persons with substance use disorders avoid future relapses by producing a therapeutic impact that helps control how the brain senses pleasure.

According to research, including meditation sessions in recovery programs may assist patients with substance dependence or addiction to regulate their impulses and lessen withdrawal symptoms.

Substance abusers who meditate regularly exhibit decreased aggressiveness and craving. They also show symptoms of increased self-awareness and recover faster than non-meditators. Although it is unclear if meditation directly helps addiction management, its effects for inducing a positive mental change in addicts are apparent and widely acknowledged.

After 3 months, practicing transcendental meditation was related to decreased levels of stress, psychological distress, alcohol cravings, and alcohol use in one research of 60 patients getting treatment for alcohol use disorder.

Meditation may also assist you in controlling your food cravings. A meta-analysis of 14 research found that meditation helped individuals minimize emotional and binge eating.

15. Meditation Reduces the Risk of Heart Diseases and Stroke

Heart disease kills more people than any other ailment in the world.

In a late-2012 research, a group of over 200 high-risk adults was randomly assigned to either a health education session emphasizing improved nutrition and exercise or a Transcendental Meditation program. Over the following 5 years, researchers who accompanied the participants discovered that those who followed the meditation class had a 48 % lower overall risk of heart attack, stroke, and death.

They found that meditation substantially lowered the risk of death, myocardial infarction, and stroke in individuals with coronary heart disease. These modifications were linked to decreased blood pressure and psychological stressors.

Other studies leading to similar results on linked health concerns have also been conducted.

16. Treats Depression

Meditation trains your mind to focus on the present moment, making it less likely that you will linger on worrisome thoughts, which may feed sadness. Studies on moderate and severe depressed patients revealed that including meditation in their normal depression care practices improved feelings of loneliness and overall poor mood.

A study of 400 Belgian teenage students found that when they engaged in meditation programs, they had a significant decrease in sadness, negative thinking, and stress for up to 6 months following the training.

According to a 2014 study published in JAMA Internal Medicine, meditation may help relieve anxiety and sadness and might be part of a complete mental health treatment strategy.

Mindfulness-based stress reduction (MBSR)—a therapeutic approach that involves meditation—has also been shown to be beneficial in studies. MBSR has been shown in studies to assist people with anxiety relax their brains and minimize symptoms of depression, such as difficulty sleeping, lack of appetite, and poor mood.

17. Regulates Anxiety and Mood Disorders

From GAD (Generalized Anxiety Disorders) to phobia, panic disorder, obsession, and bipolar mood swings, regular meditation practice aids in managing the illogical emotional ups and downs.

Methods like Vipassana diminish the density of grey matter in brain regions associated with stress and anxiety, bringing about general emotional stability.

One research discovered that 8 weeks of meditation helped people with generalized anxiety disorder decrease anxiety symptoms, increase positive self-statements, and improve stress reactivity and coping.

Another research of 47 persons with chronic pain found that following an 8-week meditation program resulted in significant reductions in depression, anxiety, and pain after over a year.

Meditation may also aid in the reduction of job-related anxiety. Employees who used a meditation app for 8 weeks had higher sentiments of well-being, less discomfort, and less work pressure than those in a control group, according to one research.

18. Provides Resilience to Pain

Your sense of pain is linked to your mental state, and it may be heightened under stressful situations.

According to some studies, including meditation in your daily practice may be good for pain management.

One analysis of 38 research, for example, showed that meditation might reduce pain, enhance the quality of life, and reduce depressive symptoms in persons with chronic pain.

Meditation was connected with reduced pain, according to a major meta-analysis of trials including over 3,500 people. Non-meditators and meditators experienced the same sources of pain, but meditators showed a stronger capacity to manage discomfort and even had a lessened awareness of pain.

19. Helps in Dealing with ADHD

Meditation has been shown to increase attention and concentration. A study of 50 adults with ADHD found that mindfulness and meditation techniques decreased hyperactivity and enabled them to have better impulse control.

Professor Eileen Lugers' brain tests at the UCLA Laboratory of Neurology-imagine revealed that meditators had greater gyrification, which helps the brain to absorb information quicker and improve selective attention and concentration.

20. The Neurological Benefits

Scientists today consider meditation to be an all-around answer to lifestyle problems, and they have presented some mind-boggling data on how meditation rewires neuronal circuits to promote inner calm and stability.

The lateral prefrontal cortex is the part of the brain that is in charge of logical reasoning and reasonable thought. According to neuropsychological research, regular meditation modulates the functioning of the lateral prefrontal cortex, giving us the feeling that we are always in "control" of our thoughts.

Meditation also has an impact on the medial prefrontal cortex, known as the "Me Center," which is the brain location responsible for our perceptions, comprehension, and knowledge. When we commit to regular meditation, we become more aware of ourselves and our surroundings, become more empathic and self-compassionate, and establish more positive relations with one another.

Meditation also affects our mental health by regulating the functioning of the ventromedial cortex, dorsomedial cortex, amygdala, and insula, which are all specialized brain centers that regulate our emotions, reactions to anxiety, fear, and bodily sensations such as pain, hunger, and thirst.

21. Induces Healthy Eating Habits

When we are in a bad mood or feel sad, we typically seek unhealthy or comfort foods that momentarily satisfy our minds. According to studies, developing morning meditation practice makes it simpler to eliminate excess sugar and fatty foods from our diet.

The pleasant energy and understanding provided by those few minutes of awareness speeds up metabolism and cleanses the gut, causing us to feel more full and less drawn to unhealthy food selections.

22. Enhances Self-Awareness

Meditation may help you get a better awareness of yourself and evolve into your best self.

Self-inquiry meditation, for example, expressly tries to help you build a better awareness of yourself and how you interact with people around you.

Other forms train you to spot potentially damaging or self-defeating beliefs. The idea is that as you become more conscious of your thinking habits, you will be able to redirect them toward more productive patterns.

A meta-analysis of 27 research found that practicing Tai Chi may be connected with increased self-efficacy, which is a person's conviction in their own capacity or ability to handle obstacles.

Another research found that 153 persons who used a meditation app for two weeks had less loneliness and more social interaction than those in a control group.

Additionally, meditation practice may help to develop more creative problem-solving abilities.

23. Generates Kindness

Meditation may help you develop compassion for yourself and others. It increases brain circuits that detect other people's emotions, increases altruistic conduct, and reduces the implicit or unconscious prejudice that is responsible for the perpetuation of negative stereotypes.

Meditation improves your emotions and behavior toward yourself and others. People learn to extend this love and forgiveness to others through practice, initially to friends, then acquaintances, and finally foes.

A meta-analysis of 22 research on meditation found that it may boost people's compassion for themselves and others.

One research of 100 people randomly allocated to a meditation program discovered that these benefits were dose-dependent. In other words, the more time individuals spent practicing meditation weekly, the better feelings they experienced.

Another research of 50 college students found that meditating

3 times per week enhanced positive emotions, interpersonal relationships, and understanding of others after 4 weeks.

These advantages also seem to increase over time with practicing meditation.

24. Improves Sleep

Almost half of the population will have insomnia at some time in their lives. Learning to meditate may help you regulate or divert the rushing or racing thoughts that frequently contribute to sleeplessness.

One research compared meditation practice and found that persons who meditated slept longer and had less severe insomnia than those who had an unmedicated control condition.

It may also assist to relax your body, reducing tension, and putting you in a pleasant state where you're more likely to fall asleep.

25. Can Decrease Blood Pressure

Meditation may also benefit physical health by lowering heart strain. High blood pressure causes the heart to work harder to pump blood, which may contribute to poor cardiac function over time.

High blood pressure also leads to atherosclerosis, or artery constriction, which may result in a heart attack or stroke.

Meditation seems to lower blood pressure in part by relaxing nerve impulses that coordinate heart function, blood vessel tightness, and the "fight-or-flight" response, which raises awareness in stressful conditions.

Meditation was shown to effectively lower blood pressure in a meta-analysis of 12 research involving over 1000 people. This worked better in older participants and those who had high blood pressure previous to the trial.

According to one study, different styles of meditation resulted in similar blood pressure improvements.

26. Reduces Activity in the Brain's "Me Center"

One of the most intriguing recent research, conducted at Yale University, discovered that meditation reduces activity in the Default Mode Network (DMN), the brain network responsible for mind-wandering and self-referential thinking, also known as "monkey mind."

When we are not thinking about something specific, our brains wander from thought to thought, the DMN is "on" or active. Many individuals want to reduce their mind-wandering since it is related to being less cheerful, ruminating, and worrying about the past and future.

Several studies have revealed that meditation, by quieting the DMN, seems to achieve precisely that. Even when the mind wanders, meditators are better at snapping back out of it because of the new connections that form.

27. Reduces Risk of Alzheimer's and Premature Death

According to the findings of a new study published online in the journal Brain, Behavior, and Immunity, simply 30 minutes of meditation every day not only decreases feelings of loneliness but also lowers the risk of heart disease, depression, Alzheimer's, and early mortality.

28. Reduces Social Anxiety and Improves Self-Esteem

Meditation is just as helpful as antidepressants in alleviating anxiety and depression symptoms. It raises the Prana (life energy) level in the body. Anxiety naturally diminishes when Prana levels rise, according to Ayurveda.

Meditation improves self-esteem by strengthening one's capacity to evaluate one's thoughts and emotions without judgment. Meditation also helps you to calm down, allows for greater self-reflection, and may assist you in discovering good aspects of yourself.

According to Stanford University experts, meditation might be particularly beneficial to those who suffer from social anxiety. In a 2009 research published in the Journal of Cognitive Psychotherapy, 14 people with social anxiety disorder completed a 2-month meditation program and reported less anxiety and higher self-esteem thereafter.

29. Long-Term Meditation Improves the Gamma Waves in the Brain

In a study with Tibetan Buddhist monks conducted by The University of Wisconsin neuroscientist Richard Davidson, it was discovered that novice meditators showed a slight increase in gamma activity, but most monks showed extremely large increases in a way that has never been reported before in neuroscience literature.

30. Improves Information Processing and Decision-Making Abilities

The UCLA Laboratory of Neuro Imaging discovered that long-term meditators had more gyrification ("folding" of the cortex, which may assist the brain to absorb information quicker) than non-meditators. Scientists believe that gyrification is responsible for increasing the brain's ability to absorb information, make decisions, form memories, and pay attention.

31. Prevents You from Multitasking Too Often

When the brain is provided with multiple objectives to pay attention to, and they are presented half a second apart (half a second difference), the second one is often missed. This is known as an "attentional-blink."

Multitasking is both a harmful productivity myth and a cause of stress. Shifting focus between activities is costly for the brain and causes emotions of distraction and unhappiness with the work at hand.

In a research conducted by the University of Washington and University of Arizona, Human Resource personnel were given 8 weeks of training in either meditation or body relaxation techniques and were given a stressful multitasking test both before and after training. The group of employees who had practiced meditation reported lower levels of stress and improved memory for the activities they had completed; they also switched activities less often and stayed focused on activities for longer periods.

32. Improves Visuospatial Processing and Working Memory

Participants' visuospatial processing, working memory, and executive functioning improved dramatically following just 4 sessions of mindfulness meditation training, according to research.

33. Increases Awareness of Your Unconscious Mind

A study conducted by researchers from the University of Sussex in the United Kingdom discovered that persons who practice meditation have a bigger pause between unconscious urges and action and are less susceptible to hypnosis.

34. Fosters Creativity

A study from Leiden University in the Netherlands found that practicing meditation improves creativity and divergent thinking. Participants who had followed the practice performed better on a task that required them to come up with fresh ideas creatively.

35. It Paves Your Way towards Spiritual Enlightenment

What exactly is spiritual awakening? Perhaps you've wondered about your spirit or soul, whether you're more than your body and mind. The instant you start asking these questions, you are on the path to spiritual awakening. It symbolizes the beginning of your quest for answers.

If you discover that what is accessible via exterior knowledge, whether from books or the internet, isn't fulfilling, you may want to discover how to go deeper by searching inside, where all wisdom awaits. Learning to meditate is a practice that might assist you in locating what you are seeking.

36. Prevents Asthma, Rheumatoid Arthritis, and Inflammatory Bowel Disease

Two groups of participants were exposed to different forms of stress management in a study done by neuroscientists at the University of Wisconsin-Madison. One was given meditation training, while the other was given dietary advice, exercise, and music therapy. The research revealed that meditation practices were more beneficial than other activities that promote well-being in reducing inflammatory symptoms.

37. Increases Feelings of Compassion and Decreases Worry

Individuals who participated in a 9-week Compassion Cultivation Programme (CCT) showed substantial gains in all 3 areas of compassion—compassion for others, compassion received from others, and self-compassion. In a similar setting, the practitioners reported a reduction in anxiety and emotional repression.

38. Is Helpful for Patients Diagnosed with Fibromyalgia

In a research published in PubMed, 11 Fibromyalgia patients undertook an 8-week meditation training program. As a result, the researchers discovered a substantial improvement in the subjects' general health condition as well as symptoms of stiffness, anxiety, and depression. Significant improvements were also seen in the reported number of days "felt good" and "missed work" due to Fibromyalgia.

39. It may even Help Treat HIV

Lymphocytes, also known as CD4 T cells, are the immune system's "brains," directing its activities when the body is attacked. They are also the cells targeted by HIV, the deadly virus that causes AIDS and has infected around 40 million people worldwide. The virus gradually destroys CD4 T cells, weakening the immune system.

However, HIV/AIDS patients' immune systems must contend with another foe like stress, which may hasten the decline of CD4 T cells. The practice of meditation, according to UCLA researchers, has prevented the loss of CD4 T cells in HIV-positive individuals who are stressed, halting the course of the illness.

Creswell and his colleagues used a stressed and racially diverse group of 48 HIV-positive people in Los Angeles to evaluate an 8-week mindfulness-based stress-reduction (MBSR) meditation program to a 1-day MBSR control seminar. Participants in the 8-week group had no reduction of CD4 T cells, showing that meditation training may help to prevent declines. The control group, on the other hand, had substantial decreases in CD4 T cells from pre-study to post-study. Such declines are a common symptom of HIV progression.

40. Meditation Helps Manage Psoriasis

Psychological stress is a powerful inflammatory trigger. A short meditation-based stress reduction therapy provided through audiotape during ultraviolet light treatment was proven to improve psoriatic lesion resolution in psoriasis patients.

41. Improves Empathy and Positive Relationships

You are less prone to blame others and engage in unpleasant emotions such as hate as your awareness develops while you meditate. Your attachment to events weakens, and you become the person who quickly forgets that little quarrel. Who doesn't like that individual? You also experience greater love in your relationships because certain techniques help release more oxytocin, the hormone that fosters emotions of love and social connection.

According to Emory University research, such activities successfully improve one's capacity to empathize with others by interpreting their facial expressions.

According to another study, the development of positive emotions through compassion builds several personal resources, including a loving attitude toward oneself and others, self-acceptance, social support received, and positive relationships with others, as well as a sense of competence about one's life, which includes pathways thinking, environmental mastery, purpose in life, and ego.

42. Reduces Social Isolation

According to a research published in the American Psychological Association, respondents who practiced meditation for only a few minutes enhanced their sentiments of social connection and optimism toward new people on both explicit and implicit levels. These findings imply that this simple strategy may assist to boost pleasant social feelings while decreasing social isolation.

43. Decreases the Feelings of Loneliness

According to a Carnegie Mellon University research, meditation may help reduce feelings of loneliness, which reduces the risk of morbidity, mortality, and the expression of pro-inflammatory genes.

44. Reduces Emotional Eating

Transcendental Meditation, according to scientists, helps control emotional eating, which helps avoid obesity.

45. You Learn to Let Go and Be Firm

When we are unable to let go of a life circumstance, it has a profound effect on us. We are tormented by the emotional baggage of a negative scenario and person. Sometimes, to the point that our capacity to live joyfully collapses. Regular meditation allows us to let go while simultaneously allowing us to remain firm and enthusiastic about what we are doing.

46. Meditation May Help You Live Longer

Telomeres are crucial components of human cells that influence how our cells mature. Though the study is in its early stages, there is evidence that some forms of meditation may have beneficial effects on telomere length by lowering cognitive stress and stress arousal and enhancing good states of mind and hormonal factors that may support telomere maintenance.

47. Reduces Aging

Meditation, according to studies, keeps you youthful and enhances your longevity. One of the key reasons for this is that it reduces stress, which has a harmful influence on the body.

48. Promotes More Energy and Efficiency

Meditation helps to clean one's thoughts and boost one's energy levels. Meditation may activate the Vagus nerve, promoting good feelings and relaxation. According to a new research, meditation reduces tiredness among entrepreneurs by reducing workplace pressures, offering you more peace and energy. As you feel more energy and have better mental clarity, your efficiency automatically rises.

49. You Find Your Purpose and Passion

Have you ever wondered how to discover your true passion?

Setting an intention to quiet your mind's chatter will help you more easily tune in to what your soul is trying to tell you about your true calling.

This will make you live a life that is a joyful expression of your highest purpose, while also feeling more inspired and passionate along the way!

50. It Improves Your Presence and Mindfulness

Meditation is an excellent approach to cultivate mindfulness.

Consistent meditation will allow you to see how your thoughts and emotions tend to move in predictable patterns.

If you establish a habit of observing what you see, your days will be filled with more self-awareness, appreciation, and thankfulness, and you will be able to choose who you will be and what you will experience at any given moment.

51. You Experience the Inner and Outer Peace of Connecting with Your Joy Within

When you are looking for solutions and are unable to find them, you may get restless or irritated. You may be looking for answers to your life's purpose, who you are, and why you are here. This restlessness is often the beginning of your spiritual awakening.

The solutions are there inside you, only waiting to be accessed via meditation practice. Learn how to enter your unique sanctuary of happiness and pleasure via meditation, which will lead to inner and outward serenity and enduring delight.

THE ROLE OF DIET
IN MEDITATION

When you sit down to meditate, do you ever feel tired or overwhelmed with a billion thoughts? It's possible that your food is to blame. Basic knowledge of food may transform the way you meditate and your life.

Food not only feeds the body but also influences the mind's alertness and consciousness. As a result, you must understand your diet, your body, and your mind.

Our food has a tremendous influence on our mental health. However, many individuals are utterly unaware of the impact diet has on their health. We eat whatever is handy or tasty without paying much attention to how it affects us.

However, when you meditate, you get more in touch with your feelings. As a result, you're more aware of which meals to consume and which to avoid. Certain meals make you feel light and joyous, while others make you feel heavy and unhappy.

Our bodies are like instruments that need to be tuned regularly. Flawless music requires a perfect instrument. Similarly, a light and healthy physique is required for excellent quality meditation. Bad eating habits, a lack of understanding about what is beneficial for our system, a lack of relaxation and healthy sleep, as well as years of abuse of body and mind, may all lead to illnesses in the body over time.

If we want to go deeper into meditation and achieve real spiritual growth, we should attempt to consume meditation-friendly meals.

So, here are some suggestions for creating a perfect meditation diet:

1. Consider Food to be Energy

The most crucial component of your meditation diet is that you start to think of food as energy. The more we can understand food as energy, the better our dietary decisions will be. But it's difficult when we've spent our whole lives eating for the purpose of eating. Analyze how everything you consume affects your body, mind, and soul.

Before you eat, assess if the meal supplies the critical life energy you need. Some foods are high in energy, while others are low in energy. As you meditate, you will become more aware of what makes you joyful and what depresses you.

Just note how you feel after eating a huge pizza or fried chicken. And how do you feel after eating a nutritious salad and some fresh fruit?

2. Drink Freshly Prepared Juices

Juicing is an excellent technique to get many high-energy meals into your system at once.

It has also grown in popularity because of its many advantages, which include weight reduction, increased energy levels, improved cognitive function, a stronger immune system, and a healthier look.

The nutrients are readily absorbed by the body and do not need to be broken down. Try it out for a few days and notice how it impacts your meditation.

3. Consume Raw or Lightly Cooked Meals

Cooking food depletes its energy. A fresh carrot has much more nutrients than a carrot that has been baked in the oven for an hour.

So, consume raw foods whenever possible, and when you must cook food, cook it very gently to retain part of its vital power.

Steaming veggies for a few minutes is preferable to boiling or baking them.

4. Limit Your Sugar Consumption

Our diets are loaded with sugar. Sugar has a Rajasic (activating) influence on consciousness, therefore it functions as a mild stimulant. As a result, it hinders inner tranquility. Sugar also contributes to a variety of health issues—such as tooth decay, weight gain, and obesity.

I don't believe it's essential to entirely cut sugar out of your diet. However, it is absolutely prudent to limit it as much as possible.

Sugar is also very addicting and harmful; thus, it may be worthwhile to try avoiding sugar for a brief period to cleanse the body.

Some of the greatest strategies to eliminate sugar from your diet are to eliminate them one at a time:

- Beverages
- Alcoholic drinks (particularly those with a sweet taste)
- Cereal
- Cakes
- Chocolate

5. Avoid Eating Meat

One of the most important aspects of a meditation diet is that we strive to avoid eating meat as much as possible. Vegetarianism has a significant influence on both your health and the environment.

Animals are alive, loving creatures; they are not food.

Do you notice how many individuals on the spiritual path begin to abstain from meat? What is the reason behind this? One of the numerous reasons is that they begin to experience the full impact of meat on their bodies and thoughts. When we meditate regularly, we become more in tune with our overall sense of well-being.

Remember that everything is made out of energy. Consider the amount of energy contained inside an animal that has been tortured for its whole existence and then dies inhumanely. This is not the place to go into detail about how much pain these creatures go through, but to suggest that a lifetime of agony is an understatement.

What happens if you consume the energy of a cow or a pig? You devour the animal's profound fear, his fury, and his pain. That becomes a part of you.

So, think twice before consuming meat, it is strictly exempted by Ayurveda. You would not believe how many harmful impacts it has on your health and psyche.

6. Experiment with Fasting

Fasting may be done in a variety of ways. You might begin with a fast in which you only eat a tiny meal or two every few hours, then fast for the remainder of the day, so you're fasting for around 20 hours and eating for 4 hours.

You might also attempt a juice fast, in which you only consume fresh fruit and vegetable juices for the whole day. In the evening, you may eat a soup made entirely of fruits and vegetables.

When you're ready, spend a whole day drinking just water. This is difficult, so work your way up. According to what I've heard, the first day or two are difficult, but you grow accustomed to it and it gets easier.

Intermittent fasting is another wonderful option. There are several reasons to do so:

- It provides a plethora of health advantages.
- It has the potential to aid with weight reduction.
- It has the potential to alter our relationship with food.
- It aids us in eating less throughout the week.
- It makes us feel lighter and invigorated.
- It removes toxins from the body.

All of this has a great influence on our meditation practice since it relaxes the mind.

7. Make a List of Your Favorite Foods

When we run out of ideas, we tend to revert to old habits and what we already know. As a result, it's a good idea to have a list of meals on hand.

Make a list of high-energy meals that you love so that you can organize your grocery shopping.

Be inventive, but remember to keep things simple. We don't need a whole fresh menu every week. In fact, if you love them, you may have several of the same meals every week.

8. Allow Ayurveda to Assist You in Making Dietary Decisions

A simple modification in your eating habits that aligns with your Prakriti allows you to have a healthier, more balanced life while also experiencing deeper meditation. To preserve our psychological equilibrium, the 3 characteristics—Tamas, Rajas, and Sattva are required. The first two operate against a mentally balanced condition. Tamasic meals (such as meat, processed meals, and alcohol) dull the intellect, while Rajasic meals (such as spicy sauce and coffee) overwhelm and overstimulate. A Sattvic diet that corresponds to one's nature or Prakriti is desirable.

Sattvic foods include freshly prepared foods as well as raw fruits and vegetables. It cleanses the mind and soothes the body.

Rajasic food is overly tasty. It stimulates both the body and the intellect. Rajasic food includes garlic and onion-flavored foods, greasy and fatty foods, coffee, tea, and spicy foods.

Tamasic foods weaken the intellect and cause confusion and negativity. Non-vegetarian, stale and fermented food, liquor, processed food, and overripe fruits and vegetables are all included.

According to Ayurvedic practitioners, the most spiritual diet is one that consists mostly of Sattvic foods. These are those that are thought to be pure and non-harmful (to yourself or others).

The more your Sattva, the deeper your meditation. So, make good eating choices to pave the way for a happy meditation session. A healthy body and a peaceful mind allow us to meditate more effectively and delve deeper into ourselves. A vegetarian diet is gentler on the body and more suited to meditation.

Sattvic foods include the following:

- Fruits and vegetables that are ripe (in season).
- Seeds and nuts.
- Original grains.
- Legumes and other plant-based proteins that have been lightly processed.
- Natural sugar substitutes (in moderation).

To create balance, it is recommended that you consume these items in equal proportions. As a result, a buddha bowl (equal parts grain, vegetables, and protein with a fat-based dressing or garnish) would be an appropriate Sattvic food.

Caffeine-rich foods work as stimulants, making the mind hyperactive. Spices with a high heat level may have a similar effect. Many items that are forbidden in Vedic cookery are also aphrodisiacs. It goes without saying that they would be detrimental to a pure mental state. Tobacco and alcohol are also self-explanatory. Processed foods (such as white flour/sugar, microwaveable or canned meals, and packaged snacks) cause brain fog and make it difficult to focus. The list goes on...

If you are serious about your meditation practice, you should restrict Tamasic and Rajasic products. It may be difficult at first, but the benefits to your meditation will undoubtedly be worth it.

Try these substitutions for the following "forbidden" foods:

- Coffee—Try chicory and/or dandelion root tea.
- Chocolate—Carob is a wonderful, milder substitute.
- Onion—Fennel or celery might have a similar flavor.
- White Sugar—Replace with brown rice syrup or stevia.
- Fried Foods—Heavy root vegetables (such as sweet potato) and/or rich healthy fats (such as nut butters) may be just as filling without the negative consequences.

It's also vital to think about what's going through your head when you're eating. Eating when stressed causes the body to get confused about where to focus its heat and energy. The flavor of the food and the desire to consume is also affected by your mood. It is best not to do anything else while eating, since your attention has to be focused on what and how much you are eating for proper and easy digestion.

Proper food and eating habits can eliminate negative thoughts, relax your mind, and increase your body's vitality, allowing you to live a better life.

9. Make Your Cooking and Eating More Spiritual

We must prepare our meals properly. Try to cook gently and joyfully. Don't go about in a frenzy. Relax and cook with love. The foods you consume will then be able to provide you with additional nutrients.

Before you eat, you might also say a prayer. This is a very powerful thing to perform. If this is unusual for you, take a minute to be appreciative of the meal. Feel gratitude for all the time and effort that went into making this delicious meal on your plate.

If you prepare and eat with love, that energy will get incorporated into you after your meal.

10. Don't Try Too Hard

If we have developed eating habits over a long period, they do not go immediately. Finding ways to improve your nutrition requires time, experience, and experimenting. Begin with tiny modifications, such as eliminating one kind of food and replacing it with another.

Be kind to yourself and take it one step at a time. Small, long-term changes are preferable to drastic, short-term ones. Make both long-term and short-term goals. If being a vegetarian is your ultimate objective, begin with omitting beef, then pork, lamb, and so on.

Similarly, start with one kind of whole grain if you wish to consume all. There's no need to stock up on buckwheat, millet, and barley at the organic shop.

Here are a Few Additional Pointers

- Prepare your meals fresh and prevent overcooking.
- If you need to reheat leftovers, use the stove or oven rather than the microwave.
- Avoid using too many spices and intricate meal combinations; instead, keep it simple.
- Try to schedule your meals strategically for optimal energy and digestion—don't avoid breakfast in the morning, eat your big meal around lunchtime, and eat dinner before 9 pm.
- Slow down—eat deliberately rather than hurriedly or anxiously.

When you eat healthily, you will notice that several things begin to happen:

- You can meditate for longer periods of time.
- You are better able to meditate regularly.
- Throughout the day, you have more energy.
- You are less sluggish.
- You have greater insight and knowledge.
- You're happier and more at ease.
- You can be more present throughout the day.

Of course, there are several other advantages to your health, mind, and soul. If you can learn to eat healthily, you notice that every aspect of your life will begin to improve. It is definitely worthwhile to put in the time and effort now.

Remember that your diet does not have to be perfect. You are evolving as long as you are conscious and making adjustments.

VARIOUS MEDITATION ASANAS

There are a million different types of meditation, yet if you took pictures of individuals meditating all across the globe, many of them would seem quite similar. Why? Because there are certain fundamental components of the meditation posture that are used all over the world to quiet the mind and align the body.

Patanjali's Yoga Sutras define yoga as having eight limbs, one of which is asana, or meditation seat. The Sutras do not specify any asanas, instead describes the qualities of a good asana.

Meditative asanas are positions that let you sit or stand comfortably for long periods, allowing you to focus and meditate without being distracted by muscular proprioceptors. The concept behind meditative asanas is to simply arrange oneself in such a manner that one's limbs stop sending impulses to the mind, enabling the practitioner to focus on meditation.

Over the centuries, meditative asanas have been referenced repeatedly in different Indian texts on yoga, including the Puranas and the Vedas, and have served as the foundation for the development of a complete physical culture of asana practice. The Lotus Pose and kneeling postures are well-known in Buddhist and Hindu traditions; other options include Sukhasana, Siddhasana, or sitting on a chair with the spine erect.

For Westerners who have not practiced sitting cross-legged since infancy, the Lotus Pose especially may be very painful. It can induce knee discomfort and injury. As a result, there are some simple asanas as well.

The cross-legged pose offers a solid foundation for meditation and has been utilized for millennia in Buddhism and Hinduism. The cross-legged poses are easy and steady, relaxing for the muscles while keeping the practitioner aware.

Other positions are also used for meditation in different religions. People who find sitting cross-legged unpleasant may sit erect on a straight-backed chair, flat-footed and without back support, with their hands resting on their thighs, a posture known as the Egyptian position. The following are some of the most popular asanas for meditation:

Sukhasana (Comfortable Pose)

This sitting position is suggested for individuals who find it difficult to sit for an extended length of time in Siddhasana, Vajrasana, or Padmasana.

How to Do:

Sit with your legs straight. Bend both legs and put the right foot on the floor beneath the left thigh and the left foot in front of the right calf. Cross your legs in the opposite direction if it is more comfortable. If keeping the body straight is difficult, sit on a cushion at an adequate height to make the posture more comfortable.

If sitting comfortably and painlessly in Sukhasana is not possible, perform the breathing and meditation techniques while sitting on a chair. The most essential thing for everyone is that the upper body is straight, that the body is relaxed, and that the body can stay immobile during the activity.

Vajrasana (Sitting on the Heels)

Vajrasana relaxes and unifies the body and mind. Because this posture promotes digestion, it is advised that you sit in Vajrasana for 5-10 minutes after eating.

How to Do:

Come onto your knees (knee stand). The legs are joined. The large toes rub together, and the heels point slightly outwards. Tilt your upper body forward and sit back between your heels. Your trunk should stand straight. Place your hands on your thighs.

Siddhasana/Ardha Padmasana (Pose

of the Adept/Half Lotus)

This posture is suggested for individuals who find it difficult to sit comfortably in Padmasana. It calms the mind, balances the Nadis (nerves), and awakens the spiritual energy of the Chakras. As a result, this sitting position is ideal for practicing Pranayama and Meditation.

How to Do:

Sit up straight with your legs spread. Bend the right leg and put the foot on the floor very near to the body. Bend your left leg and put your left foot on top of your right calf. The sole of the foot makes contact with the right thigh. Pull the right foot's toes up between the thigh and the calf of the left leg, and the left foot's toes down between the thigh and the calf of the right leg. Sit on a cushion at the proper height if it is difficult to maintain the body upright or the knees do not rest on the floor.

This posture may also be practiced by bending the left leg first and bringing the right foot along the left calf.

Padmasana (Lotus Pose)

Padmasana, together with Sirsasana (Headstand), is known as the ultimate or "Royal" asana. The Lotus Pose stimulates and balances the Chakras while also silencing the mind. It is an excellent sitting position for Pranayama and Meditation.

It is an excellent sitting position for Pranayama and Meditation.

How to Do:

Sit on the floor with your legs straight. Bend the right leg and put the foot on top of the left thigh, very close to the body. Bend the left leg and place the foot on top of the right thigh, very close to the body. The upper body should be fully erect, with the knees touching the floor. Sit on a cushion of an adequate height to help keep the trunk upright and the knees on the floor.

This posture may also be performed by bending the left leg first, followed by the right.

You may meditate in any of these asanas while paying close attention to the components mentioned below:

Body Alignment: Align the back, neck, and head in an upright and comfortable position while sitting in meditation postures. Avoid hunching or leaning. Sit upright, with a gentle smile on your face. Those who have trouble sitting on the floor may use a meditation cushion to cushion themselves. Make sure you double-check the alignment and adjustment.

Relaxation: Relax the body's muscles and joints. In any posture, do not strain your neck, shoulders, knees, or arms. With hands on the lap, the arms should be easily stretched out.

Stillness: Develop a feeling of balance and steadiness. Rock side and forth until you locate your center of balance. Keep your eyes closed to concentrate on your Third Eye.

VARIOUS MEDITATION MUDRAS

Our hands have a unique role in our lives. We use them to eat, welcome people, do everyday tasks, communicate, create, and express love. The hands are regarded as significant energy centers in yoga, martial arts, and South Indian dance traditions; in Ayurveda and traditional Chinese medicine, the various fingers are linked with various organs, helping to regulate our health.

Hasta Mudras, which translate to "seals, stamps, or gestures," are holy hand motions that have been utilized for thousands of years in many faiths to deepen one's practice and awaken the power of the Divine. Today, Hasta Mudras are vital tools for freeing up energy (Prana) and directing it to parts of the body that need healing. Every mudra has a specific function and directs energy in a certain direction throughout the body to produce subtle physical, mental, and emotional changes.

If you arrive at your meditation practice feeling angry or worried, for example, putting your hands face down on your thighs can typically quiet and center your energy. If you're feeling sluggish or drowsy, try a palms-up mudra.

As a result, it makes sense that Hasta Mudras may assist you in positively directing your thoughts and actions to bring beauty into your life and the world around you. Mudras can assist you in evoking the presence of a great goddess inside you so she may physically strengthen you, enabling you to experience her energy and echo her speech. With this particular experience etched in your heart, you will be able to be your real, powerful self.

The hands, as action organs and sense receptors, have a close relationship with the brain, both via neuronal activity and on more subtle levels. This implies that how we hold our hands may affect how we hold our minds. And it is for this reason that yogis have performed hand mudras, or gestures, for millennia.

The goal of yoga is to bring oneself within. Mudras enable us to go inside and refuel our batteries. Over the years, more than a hundred mudras have been developed. A mudra may be used to help prepare the mind for meditation.

Statues depicting ancient yogis, gods, and goddesses sitting in meditation and holding their hands in various postures are common.

Yoga mudras are also regarded as a healing modality, since they are unique and based on Ayurvedic principles. A mudra can involve the whole body or be as basic as a hand posture. Mudras, when combined with yoga breathing techniques, invigorate the flow of Prana in the body, activating various areas of the body.

How do Yoga Mudras Work?

Diseases, according to Ayurveda, are caused by an imbalance in the body, which is produced by a lack or excess of any of the 5 elements.

These components are present in our fingers, and each of these 5 components performs a distinct and essential role inside the body. The fingers are, in essence, electrical circuits. Mudras are used to alter the flow of energy, altering the equilibrium of air, fire, water, earth, and ether, and promote healing.

Yoga, Buddhism, and other spiritual traditions teach that all reality is made up of 5 elements called collectively as Tattvas —earth, air, fire, water, and space (or ether)—and that their connection explains how all cosmic existence unfolds. Within

47

each of us is a heavenly composition at work. You have the limitless governing force of the cosmos inside you. Mudras are a great instrument for bringing harmony among the internal Tattvas and assisting you in focusing on whatever part of your life is problematic.

Each finger on each hand relates to and balances a distinct Tattva, according to Ayurveda. When you make a mudra, your fingers form an energy circuit that links and stimulates the components connected with the Tattvas you want to activate.

The thumb represents space, the index finger represents air, the middle finger represents fire, the ring finger represents water, and the pinky represents earth. As a result, it is thought that by generating various mudras with your hands via various finger configurations, you are tapping into that tremendous energy.

The warmth of the breath is provided by the thumb, which relates to fire. When the index finger (air element) touches the thumb, it increases the movement of the breath throughout the body; the middle finger (space or ether) and the thumb together increase spaciousness; the ring finger (earth)-thumb connection (also known as Mother Earth Mudra) brings stability; and finally, the pinky finger (water element) joining with the thumb can improve circulation.

Mudras establish a delicate link with the brain's instinctive rhythms and affect the unconscious responses in these regions. In turn, the internal energy is balanced and redirected, causing changes in the sensory organs, glands, veins, and tendons.

Yoga mudras are performed while sitting cross-legged in Vajrasana or Lotus Pose, or even while sitting comfortably on a chair. Most mudras should be practiced with Ujjayi Breathing. Take at least 12 breaths in each yoga mudra and pay close attention to the flow of energy in your body.

They are not difficult to implement, and you can begin reaping the health advantages as soon as you do. Mudras, in a nutshell, are hand postures employed during meditation to promote particular therapeutic states of mind. They assist in drawing your awareness inside and reconnecting you with the language of your heart, which is compassion, love, goodness, creativity, and joy.

Whether you're new to meditation or an experienced yogi, try out the following mudras anytime you want to take your practice to the next level.

Use these 8 revitalizing mudras to boost your mental clarity, energy, and general wellness. These hand gestures may alter your yoga asana experience, get the prana flowing, and perhaps awaken a deeper sense of self-awareness.

1. Jnana/Gyan Mudra

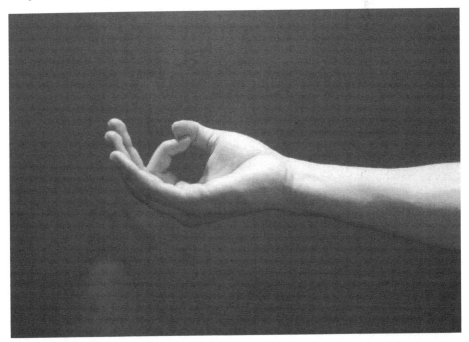

Meaning: Wisdom/Increasing awareness

Benefits: The Mudra is probably one you've seen a million times before, since it appears in every single picture of someone meditating in mainstream media. However, just because something is simple does not imply it should be ignored. Its purpose is to help you concentrate and increase your awareness and understanding. If you have a meeting or presentation coming up and need to remember things, or if you have a mental block, this is your mudra. It's also a simple and effective method to recall that you have access to an inner fountain of wisdom right inside you.

How to Do: Curl your index fingers toward the base of your thumbs to create a circle. The rest of your fingers are still pointing straight out. Then, with your hands facing up or down, place them on your knees.

2. Prana Mudra

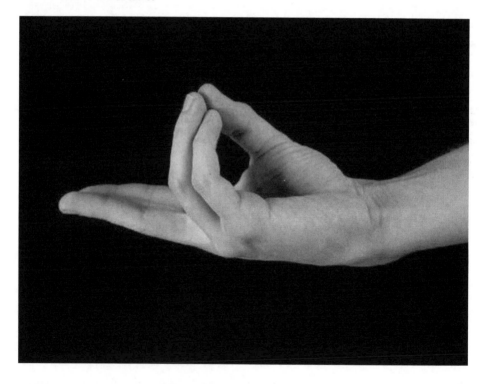

Meaning: The vital life energy

Benefits: The prana mudra opens up pathways of energy. This mudra is a wonderful addition to your morning routine to activate any latent energy.

How to Do: Connect the tip of your thumb with the tips of your ring and little finger.

3. Varada Mudra

Meaning: Granting of wishes

Benefits: "Varada mudra entails kindness, charity, giving, compassion, being part of the solution, and contributing to human salvation. Do this mudra anytime you want to impart positive feelings and compassion.

How to Do: Form the mudra by placing your left hand on your left knee, palm up and fingers extended. With your right hand, you may do the mudra shown in the image, a different mudra, or just put it on your lap, thigh, or knee.

4. Shuni Mudra

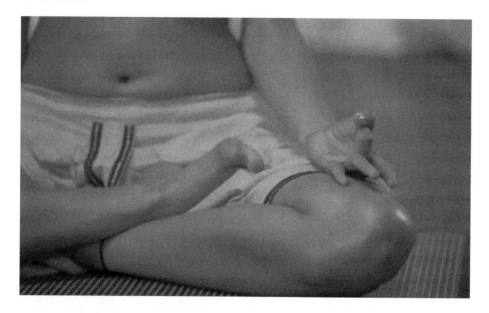

Meaning: Enhancing intuition

Benefits: This mudra is for you if you want clarity and insight into your next actions and how to execute them effectively. The Shuni Mudra brings in that concentrated attention and purpose by using the fire element inside you.

How to Do: With the tip of your middle finger, press the tip of your thumb.

5. Karana Mudra

Meaning: Keeping evil at bay

Benefits: Try this mudra for a burst of happiness when unpleasant emotions and thoughts have gotten stuck and you are unable to shake them off. There will be an almost instantaneous improvement in your mental landscape—calm, clarity, and simplicity.

How to Do: Your thumb should touch the middle and ring fingers on your right hand, and your index and pinky should be stretched. (It resembles a "rock on" hand signal.) Then, with your palm facing out, place your hand right in front of your heart. Meanwhile, your left hand may rest on your lap, palm up.

6. Apana Mudra

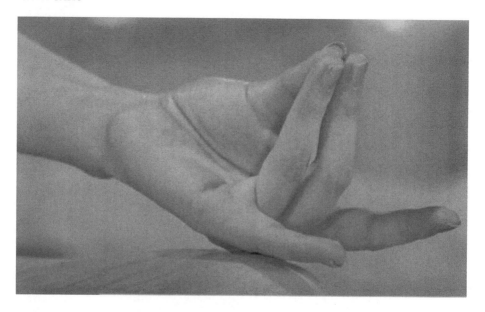

Meaning: Toxins removal

Benefits: The Apana Mudra helps control the energy in your lower belly, which controls the outward flow of energy in the body. It may aid in physical or emotional digestion by assisting in the elimination of unnecessary materials from the body.

How to Do: In the same manner as the Karana Mudra, touch the tip of your thumb to the tip of your middle and ring fingers while leaving your other two fingers extended. Then, with your hands facing up, place them on your knees.

7. Varuna Mudra

Meaning: Balance water element in the body

Benefits: This mudra may assist with constipation or indigestion. However, don't forget to take your daily probiotic prescription, drink lots of water, eat mainly a healthy, plant-based diet, and get enough sleep. In other words, think of the mudra as a digestion aid rather than a cure.

How to Do: Touch the tip of your thumbs with pinkies while keeping your other three fingers stretched out. Then, on your knees, put your hands facing up.

8. Samadhi/Dhyana Mudra

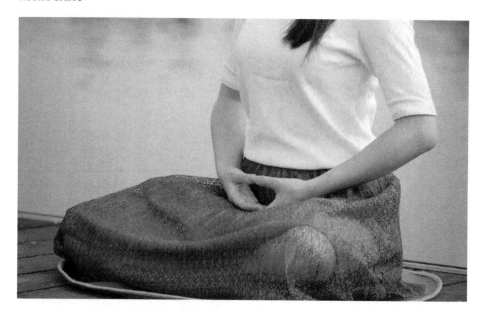

Meaning: A completely focused state

Benefits: The Buddha often performs the Samadhi Mudra, also known as the Dhyana Mudra. It promotes profound attention and clarity of focus. So, if your attention is being drawn in a million different ways and you're multitasking but still not getting much done, this is the one to try.

How to Do: Place both hands on your lap, palms facing up, and your right hand on top of your left. Touch the tips of your thumbs together lightly.

THE IDEAL SETTING FOR MEDITATION

We have a kitchen and a bedroom where we eat and sleep. It makes sense to devote a place to meditation if we want to cultivate calmness and improve our practice.

Imagine a room in your house that cures your mind, body, and soul. Wouldn't it be wonderful to have a separate space inside (or outside) your house dedicated to peace, serenity, and your mental well-being? A space where you can get away from the pressures of everyday life and connect with greater power? A meditation room will provide you with a space to accomplish just that, where you can do meditation instead of going to a studio.

Our homes are a carefully selected collection of dedicated spaces, so if meditation is part of your daily routine (or you want it to be), designating a meditation room makes perfect sense.

It's easy to make excuses for not practicing something because we don't believe we have enough space or there are too many distractions, but creating a sanctuary—no matter how tiny—can inspire you to pursue your practice and calm your soul every time you enter that place.

I believe that everyone should make a place in their homes for daily meditation; a space that allows you to refresh your body both physically and mentally, as well as keep you balanced.

Creating a quiet and distraction-free environment at home can assist the mind to settle down and remain focused. Furthermore, if you meditate in the same spot frequently, you will begin to fill that part of your house with a calming vibe. Merely by walking upon your mat (before you begin your practice), you will notice that you begin to breathe deeper simply by association.

The advantages of meditation are widely recognized; all findings to date show that meditation has a unique therapeutic and transforming potential. According to certain research, meditation can alter the way our brains function.

There are no hard and fast rules for creating a meditation space at home, but there are certain things to keep in mind. In my experience, you don't need much; in fact, less is often more. Simply thinking about what feels good to you is a fantastic beginning point for building the ideal meditation environment.

Then allow yourself to be led by what feeds your senses. Assuming you are at home, choose the room in which you feel the most comfortable or unbothered.

Take some ideas from the list below. 12 tips to design your own meditation space, but most importantly, listen to your mind and heart, only including things that you enjoy—elements that generate a personal sense of zen-like serenity.

1. Choose a Feel-Good Space

You should choose a space in your house that brings you joy. This is a space that makes you happy the moment you step in. Furthermore, you want it to be a peaceful area in the home, with little to no traffic.

When selecting a space, consider the lighting as well. A room with a lot of natural light, for example, can immediately improve your mood. This implies you should pick a space that faces the sun during the time of day you want to meditate. Or, even better, a room with a sunset view—what a lovely way to begin meditation!

If you can't locate a 'room' with these characteristics, try an outside area. This may be your patio, deck, or perhaps your flower garden. You want a location where you can rest your mind and body without being distracted.

2. Keep It Clean and Embrace Minimal Décor

When it comes to distractions, nothing beats a crowded environment, particularly when you're attempting to relax. You want to keep the number of 'extras' in the room to a minimum.

This implies you shouldn't attempt to set up a meditation area in your workplace. There is too much going on in the area with a desk, documents, file cabinets, and the stressful thoughts that come with what is in an office—work, bills, and so on.

Consider emptying the room so that just a few items remain. A modest table, a yoga mat, a throw rug, and a meditation cushion are some basic suggestions.

3. Cozy It Up

You should be at ease in your meditation space—after all, sitting cross-legged isn't always as relaxing as you would imagine. Place plush pillows, cushions, and blankets in your area to provide yourself with a comfortable sitting.

4. Try Aromatherapy

Aromatherapy is another thing to think about for your meditation space. Essential oils derived from plants, such as lavender, chamomile, and peppermint, may calm the soul, mind, and body.

While meditating, you may get the advantages of aromatherapy by lighting candles and incense or heating oils. Aromatherapy not only helps you relax, but it also has significant benefits. This kind of treatment is gaining popularity and is on its way to becoming a mainstream therapeutic tool that is thought to enhance brain activity.

There is also evidence that it strengthens the immune system, alleviates muscular discomfort, and lowers or eliminates stress. These are all excellent reasons to incorporate aromatherapy in your meditation space.

5. Bring Nature into Your Meditation Room

Nature is naturally soothing and therapeutic; therefore, it makes sense that you include some natural components into the space where you wish to relax and meditate. In fact, most people think that meditation is all about connecting your mind and body to nature and your surroundings. While it would be great to meditate outdoors in a peaceful, natural setting, this is not always feasible if you live in a bustling city.

Thus, consider incorporating natural elements into your meditation space—it will be immediately imbued with harmony and balance. You may use any natural components you want. A plant (think the smell of jasmine), a vase of flowers, jars filled with sand and seashells, or even a tiny water fountain could be used.

In fact, a water fountain is an absolute need in every meditation room. If you can't meditate on the beach while listening to the shifting ocean tides, a tiny inside waterfall will provide comparable calming sounds (and will drown out the sounds of the bustling city outside your doors).

6. Add a Personal Touch

You should certainly add some of your own unique touches while designing your meditation space. This may be any element, smell, sound, or item that specifically calms and relaxes your body and mind.

Consider bells, chimes, crystals, affirmation stones, beads, and artwork. Any of these are excellent factors for establishing a quiet and peaceful atmosphere in which you may concentrate only on meditating.

However, keep in mind that you do not want to overcrowd the area. It is crucial to maintain a clean and clear atmosphere to keep your mind open. Choose just a few pieces at a time and switch them out for new ones every now and then if you can't decide.

7. Play Meditative Music

Though this is not mandatory, music may be extremely soothing for many people. This is especially useful for people who live in a busy city, where the noises of traffic, trains, and sirens are frequently heard through the walls.

Gently played in the background, meditation music may help drown out all other distractions inside the house, enabling you to achieve a calm and peaceful state when meditating—similar to the sound of a water fountain.

When it comes to music, it is suggested that you choose music without lyrics. It does not have to be classical music, but any sounds that you find relaxing, such as ocean sounds, birds tweeting, or wind whistling. Make sure the songs are long enough to last the duration of your meditation session and consider putting the music on repeat to prevent interruption. Otherwise, you may keep it simple by meditating without any music! The decision is entirely yours.

In my opinion, meditation should always be done without music! In beginning, you can opt for music, but with time you should try meditating without music because the purpose of meditation is to be with oneself and explore the hidden treasures inside you which can only happen when you observe your mind attentively.

8. Fresh Air is Essential

Aside from the aromatherapy fragrances in the room, you should also make sure you have fresh air. Fresh air offers many advantages, like increasing your brainpower, enhancing your general health, and making you feel more rejuvenated.

This will not be difficult to acquire if your place is outside. If you are inside, make sure the space is well-ventilated and that you have the chance to catch a cool breeze now and again.

Consider bringing in a standing fan that also acts as an air purifier if you are in a room with no windows or ceiling fans. Choose one with 'quiet' technology to avoid interfering with your tranquil sounds, if you're using any.

9. Lighting Makes a Difference

As previously said, the best-case situation is to locate a room with plenty of natural light. However, window coverings are required to keep the space feeling cozy. It is suggested that you choose a sheer material in a light shade to absorb the light.

If the space you pick lacks natural light, you should pay special attention to the light fixtures you choose. You may choose dim or bright lighting, depending on your preferences. Because your attitude may vary from day to day, make sure you have access to both choices.

If you've selected an outdoor location, make sure it's not too bright from the sun during the time you want to meditate. Try to make a shade with an umbrella or a structure that enables you to hang sheer curtains if at all feasible. This will prevent the sun from hurting your eyes and keeping your mind too alert.

10. No Technology Allowed

While there are no hard and fast rules for designing a meditation room, we do want to establish one hard and fast rule: no gadgets other than your music player. This implies that phones are not permitted. Say no to phones in the meditation room to avoid the distracting 'ping' of text messages, emails, and phone calls.

When you meditate, you want to be able to "get away from it all," and a phone will not allow you to do so.

Aside from phones, it is advisable to avoid other gadgets such as video game consoles and televisions. While you may love resting in front of the television, this is not the kind of relaxation you want during meditation.

11. Eliminate Distractions

Distractions may be an issue when you have family, roommates, or co-workers around. Take proactive measures to avoid them. Seek the uninterrupted time you need from others around you.

You cannot quiet the world, no matter how hard you try. Unexpected and unwelcome events will occur in life. A neighbor may decide to mow the grass, or an irritated motorist may use the horn. You can't control everything in the outside world, but you can control what's within your head.

Develop a mindset that accepts the situation for what it is. When things don't go as planned, meditation may be an excellent practice ground for maintaining serenity, concentration, and acceptance. Allow interruptions to arise. Just be a mere observer of them and then return your focus to your meditation.

12. Take It with You

There will be something about your place that makes it seem unique and welcoming. If you know you'll be away from home for an extended period of time, try bringing a little piece of it with you. It may be a picture, an essential oil, or a holy text. When you have something familiar in your temporary space, your mind and body will be able to relax into the experience more easily, even when you are away from home.

Some Outdoor Places You can Choose

to Meditate to Change Things Up

It is beneficial to have your own meditation space, although it is not compulsory. You may meditate anywhere you want. A garden, at work, a car (if you aren't driving), or even an airport as you wait for your flight are all examples.

A peaceful room is ideal, but there are lots of alternative options available. The greatest places aren't always the most exotic; they're the ones where you can let your inner explorer wander freely.

Here are 4 meditation spots that I personally enjoy:

Gardens

Mother Nature provides a plethora of retreats for the meditator. Changing your meditation location every now and then is a wonderful way to mix things up—after all, "a change is as good as a rest." Fresh air, birds singing, heightened sense of connection and harmony with other living creatures—the garden or park will quickly get to the top of your list of ideal locations to meditate. Furthermore, research indicates that grounding, or coming into direct touch with the soil, has unexpected advantages for both physical and mental health.

Holy Places

Whether you are religious or not, meditating in a sacred location is a wonderful way to rejuvenate the soul. Sacred places that encourage introspection and connection include churches, temples, and mosques. Because of their strong spiritual energy, some meditators seek out shrines. Look for a sacred location with a serene environment that is appropriate for your practice.

Buddhist practitioners often seek out locations where renowned meditators of the past practiced. These locations are often found in isolated regions that are brimming with the spirit of meditation. Such places, whether caves in the mountains or hermitages in the woods are seen to be especially conducive to practice.

Near Rivers, Streams, and Fountains

Some of the finest places for meditation are along the banks of rivers and streams. The soothing sound of flowing water is ideal for meditation because it relaxes the mind and encourages it to stay in the present moment. Allow the stream of thoughts in your mind to flow in the same way when you meditate near flowing water—in a continuous, unobstructed manner. You should not attach to, judge, reject, or adhere to your thoughts. Simply acknowledge them as they come and let them go, like beautiful autumn leaves drifting by on a stream.

A Rooftop, Patio, or Balcony

If you want to change up your routine, roofs, patios, and balconies are excellent alternatives to your indoor meditation space. Rooftops, in particular, are ideal places to sit when they are secure and accessible. Simply climb up, sit down, and soak in the early sun while practicing meditation. This not only provides a feeling of peace and tranquillity, but it also increases your vitamin D intake. Bring some water as well as a meditation mat and cushion. You may even meditate on your rooftop at night and enjoy the peace as the rest of the world goes about its routine below.

THE EASIEST MEDITATION PRACTICE

There is one element of meditation that is so essential, if it is ignored, meditation can barely be considered having taken place at all. That essential aspect is the process of being an inner witness, a neutral observer of the mind.

Like a pedestrian stopped at a railroad crossing, watching a train pass by, meditators observe the mind from a distance. In the process, their consciousness is permeated by an unimpassioned connection with whatever comes before it. Unless this fundamental technique of dispassionate self-observation is understood and put to action, meditation will prove to be nothing but a fantasy, and our experience with it not much more than a fabrication of the mind.

There's a simple and effective meditation practice called witnessing. It is nothing but awareness in everyday tasks. It is not only a beneficial exercise for spiritual searchers seeking spiritual enlightenment but is also a wonderful practice to enhance mental tranquility in general. But the core of the witness meditation needs to be grasped before one begins to practice it.

One method to break free of attachment is to develop the witnessing awareness, to become a neutral spectator of your own life. The witness seat within you is basic awareness, the part of you that is aware of everything—simply observing, watching, not judging, just being present, being here now.

A witness is a first-hand observer. Sakshi (saa-kshe) is a Sanskrit term formed from the meanings of its two parts: Sa, which means "with," and Aksha, which means "senses or eyes." Sakshi is the ability of consciousness to detach from its connection with thoughts while still seeing them "with its own eyes."

The witness is another dimension of awareness. It coexists with your regular consciousness as another layer of awareness, as the part of you that is awake. Humans have this remarkable capacity to be in two states of awareness at once. Witnessing oneself is like shining a flashlight's beam back at oneself. In every sensory, emotional, or conceptual experience, there is the experience, the sensory, emotional, or thought data, and your knowledge of it.

We may not realize it, yet every one of us is capable of becoming such an inner witness. We may observe our mind's processes first-hand while remaining detached from them. To do so, though, we must learn to see things from Sakshi's point of view.

The term Aksha, like other Sanskrit words, has many meanings. It may also imply "the center of a wheel" in addition to its fundamental meaning. When a wheel spins, its spokes circle and its outer rim rotate, but its center, or hub, remains still. Sakshi's ability to stay calm and focused of changing circumstances is a significant trait.

As consciousness withdraws from the ever-changing landscape of body, breath, and thought, it finds rest in its own nature. And, over time, this new viewpoint is progressively absorbed until it becomes a source of spiritual power.

The term Aksha also means "spiritual knowledge," which refers to the understanding obtained by waking the Sakshi.

Your awareness of your thoughts, feelings, and emotions is the witness. Witnessing is like waking up in the morning and then looking in the mirror and seeing oneself—not judging or condemning, but just witnessing the quality of being awake. Stepping back takes you out of being immersed in your experiences, thoughts, and sensory input and into self-awareness.

That is the witness, the consciousness, and you may plant that awareness in your being's soil.

Along with self-awareness comes the subtle pleasure of just being here, living, and present in this moment. Eventually, when you float in that subjective awareness, the objects of awareness will vanish and you will enter the spiritual Self, the Atman, which is pure consciousness, joy, compassion, and the One.

The witness serves as a focusing device for you. It serves as a guide for the work you perform on yourself. You may free yourself from attachments once you realize there is a space in you that is not attached. Everything we see in the universe is a mirror of our attachments.

"Lay not up for yourselves treasures on earth, where moth and rust doth corrupt," Jesus cautioned. "For where your treasure is, there will also be your heart." Desire builds your reality; that's how it works.

Thus, the witnessing process includes 3 key components: observing our inner experience directly but from a distance, being detached and stable in the process, and eventually internalizing this experience in the shape of a new spiritual vision via meditation.

The first stage is to learn to distinguish between awareness and awareness's contents. A content of consciousness is anything that is noticed in the mind, body, or external environment. When you first begin witnessing, you may often confuse an object of awareness for the subject. This is due to people's strong identification with the objects of awareness. You must rise above each thought, emotion, and experience to avoid being associated with the contents.

The method was popularised by the Indian mystic Osho, who described meditation as "just being, just watching. Being is not doing, and neither is observing. You sit quietly doing nothing, observing whatever is going on. Thoughts will be racing through your head; your body may be tense in certain places, and you may be suffering from a migraine. Just be a bystander. Don't identify with it. Watch, be a watcher on the hills, while everything else in the valley is occurring. It's a skill, not an art."

Meditation, he claims, is not a science. It's not an art; it's a knack—exactly like that. All you need is a little patience.

The old habits will persist, and the thoughts will continue to race. And your mind is constantly in rush hour, with traffic jams. Your body isn't used to sitting quietly, so you'll be tossing and turning. There is nothing to be concerned about. Just observe how the body tosses and turns, how the mind whirls, how it is full of thoughts—consistent, inconsistent, meaningless—fantasies, dreams. You stay in the middle, simply watching.

All the world's religions have instructed individuals to do something: to halt the process of thinking, to push the body into a steady state. Yoga is a lengthy practice of pushing the body to remain motionless. A forced body, on the other hand, is not still. And all religions' prayers, meditations, and contemplations do the same thing to the mind: they compel it, they don't allow the thoughts to flow. Yes, you can do so. And if you persist, you may halt the thinking process. But this isn't the real thing; it's a complete forgery.

It is wonderful when stillness arrives on its own, when silence falls without your effort, when you observe thoughts and a time comes when thoughts start leaving and silence begins to happen. If you don't identify, if you stay a witness and don't declare, "This is my thinking," the thoughts will cease on their own.

If you remark, "This should be there..." and "This should not be there..." Then you're not a witness; you have biases and views. A witness has no bias and no judgment. He just sees in the same way that a mirror does.

When you place anything in front of a mirror, it just reflects. There is no judgment that the guy is unattractive, lovely, or that, "Aha! What a great nose you have." The mirror says nothing. Its nature is to reflect; it reflects. This is what I mean by meditation: just mirroring everything inside or outside.

And I assure you... I can promise that since it has occurred to me and many people; just wait patiently—maybe a few days, perhaps a few months, perhaps a few years. There is no way to tell since each person has a unique pattern.

You've probably seen individuals collecting antiques and postal stamps. Everyone has a distinct collection; the amount may vary, and therefore the time required may differ—but continue to be a witness as often as you can. And no particular time is required for this meditation. You can wash the floor while quietly watching yourself do so.

You can move your hand instinctively, without knowing about it, or you can move it fully conscious. There is also a qualitative difference. It is mechanical when you move it subconsciously. There is elegance when you move it with awareness. Even in your hand, which is a part of your body, you will experience calmness and coolness—what about your mind?

Slowly, as you continue to watch, the flood of thoughts begins to diminish. Moments of silence emerge; a thought appears, followed by silence before another thought arises. These gaps will provide you with your first sight of meditation as well as your first sense of relief that you have arrived home.

Soon, the gaps will get wider, and eventually, the gap will always be with you. You may be doing something, yet there is silence. You may be doing nothing, yet the silence is present. Even while you're sleeping, you can hear the silence.

The Process of Witnessing

You mustn't get confused by the terminology used to explain the witnessing process. The Sakshi is not some alien or hidden part of your consciousness tucked away in a corner of your mind. Witnessing your thoughts and feelings is neither distortion nor a biased manipulation of your consciousness.

The awareness you use to observe your thoughts and inner

experiences is essentially the same as the awareness you use to read this text. The Sakshi is the same consciousness as before, but it is free of its normal web of entanglements and attachments. Becoming this inner witness in meditation starts with learning how to surf the emotions that we usually have to live and seek them from a more detached point of view. As the rigidity of our attachments softens and we remove ourselves from them, awareness takes on a new inner feel. It becomes more peaceful, translucent, and spacious. This is your True Self. To put it another way, you are the inner witness. With each meditation, this awareness becomes deeper.

How does the self-witnessing process occur? If you wanted to witness a Thanksgiving parade, you'd want to have a good vantage position from which to do so. The location of your observation point would influence how effectively you could see and hear the passing floats and marching bands. Similarly (though more abstractly), the news sources you choose to follow events serve as a vantage point from which you view the world with some detachment. Your daily newspaper not only sharpens but also broadens your view.

Meditation serves the same purpose. During meditation, your awareness is provided a vantage point from which to watch the activities of your mind. This vantage point is provided by mindfulness, and while you relax in your focus, you may observe the actions of your mind's harmony. That is the secret to effective meditation.

Many people use breath, a mantra, or both to be the center of their attention during meditation; there's nothing wrong in it, but being attached and struggling to keep their focus on them makes it miserable rather than cultivating peacefulness. While your mind is focused on something, its regular activities (caused by anything from ordinary involvements to deep-seated and unconscious attachments) disrupt your attention. They cause the mind to lose concentration and drift from thought to thought, experience to experience. Then, rather than "seeing" experience, consciousness just participates and identifies with the wandering mind.

When you witness, on the other hand, thoughts and experiences (other than your awareness) stand out in contrast to the mind's focus, like clouds in a blue sky. As you learn to notice these fleeting thoughts without chasing them, your connection with them progressively changes. The mind gets more concentrated in its awareness over time, it develops a taste for being aware. As a result, the process of inner witnessing, or watching the mind's activities from a distance, grows stronger.

From Experience

As important as it is to keep witnessing during meditation, don't approach it too rigidly. The reservoir of thoughts, emotions, habits, and experiences stored in the mind has its own energy, and rigorously repressing it simply encourages it to re-emerge, sometimes with much greater intensity. Thus, witnessing in meditation is a balancing act in which the energy of the personality is progressively gathered and concentrated, while distractions are skilfully dealt with as they arise.

A fresh vision, a lasting mental experience, is fostered by the tranquil influence of the Sakshi, the witnessing consciousness. We learn, like the ugly duckling finds itself to be a swan, that our transitory mental patterns are not the ultimate version of ourselves—that, in the end, we are something more than our thoughts. When we experience things through the eyes of the inner witness, we feel ourselves to be that witness, that we are awareness, and that awareness is, by definition, blissful.

As the poet Tagore pointed out, our fleeting thoughts are more like approximations that need to be corrected than to reality. The inner witness assures us that our flaws and distracted thoughts do not define who we are. The inner witness, which is awakened by mindfulness, reinforced by non-attachment, and developed over the course of daily practice, provides us with a fresh perspective on ourselves.

The Practice

Time Required: 15-30 minutes, or longer if you like

What You Need:

- A precious human body-mind.
- A quiet place to practice.
- A mat and some back support (if using).
- An earplug for additional silence during the practice (optional).

How to Do:

1. Sit up straight with whichever posture and mudra you like, on a meditation cushion if desired, with your head comfortably balanced on top of your spine. Close your eyes and tilt your gaze downward slightly.

2. Take two deep, leisurely, and delightfully soft breaths. Feel a rise in your abdomen as you inhale. As you exhale, observe how your abdomen returns to a neutral posture. Repeat this 6-7 times, releasing any extra tension in your face, neck, throat, or shoulders with each breath. Gently smile.

3. Relax your body and pay attention to your breathing as though your whole body is breathing.

4. Turn your focus inside and notice the contents of your mind —the internal chattering, or mental debate, as well as the visuals flashing across that internal screen.

5. In this practice, we'll simply refer to the thoughts that arise as "thinking" and the visuals that arise as "image." We'll call the intervals between thoughts and images "rest" when neither is present.

6. So, every 5-10 seconds, just remind yourself quietly what's going on in your head. If it's just thoughts or internal conversation, just mention "thinking." Simply mention "image" if what is emerging is an image. If no thoughts or images arise, just mention "rest."

7. Distracting thoughts should be observed without responding to them. When you get caught up in a stream of thought, just recognize it and return to observing. Allow yourself to be soothed by the Sound of Silence (the hymn sound we hear when there is complete silence).

8. Continue to feel the cleaning process in your mind as you go. Loosen the energy tied up in distracting thoughts. Relax your effort and stay mindful.

9. Take note of the part of your Self that is observing and labeling your thoughts and images. This is known as the Witness Consciousness, and it is the part of consciousness that is unaffected by its contents—by the thoughts and images that arise inside it. A common metaphor for this witnessing consciousness is that it is comparable to the deepest parts of an ocean, which stays peaceful, quiet, and silent even while waves (of thought, emotion, or feeling) are roaring on the surface. Another common metaphor for the Witness is the smooth surface of a mirror, on which thoughts, internal images, perceptions, and feelings emerge, like reflections inside the mirror.

10. Feel the presence of your True Self. See yourself as the universal awareness that you are, as your witnessing ability increases over time. You are the consciousness that is witnessing. You are more than just your mind and the thoughts that go through it. Consciousness is your natural state—clear, happy, and liberated.

11. Continue to meditate for as long as you like. When your mind becomes tired, it is time to end the meditation. When you're ready to call it a session, take a few more deep, leisurely breaths, your abdomen rising with each inhale and relaxing back with each

exhalation. Note how you feel, and then gradually open your eyes. Then, deepen your breathing somewhat and gradually draw your attention back and forth.

Tips:

- If your mind wanders, don't blame yourself for it; simply return your attention to the practice.
- If you're stressed out throughout the day, spending even a minute or two to do this practice may help you reach a state of inner calmness, touch higher frequencies, and cultivate spaciousness.
- Try to keep your body, hands, finger as still as possible. Over time during the session, you'll lose sensations of various parts of your body and will better grasp the idea of you not being the body and enhancing your witnessing ability.

SOME TIPS TO BOOST YOUR MEDITATION PRACTICE

Many things, such as noises, external distractions, stress, or bodily strain, may disrupt meditation. Lack of concentration and motivation can also play a role. In this section, I'd like to provide a few ideas to help you enhance your meditation experience.

Remember that persistence and repeated practice enhance any skill, including meditation.

Here are some excellent meditation tips to help you meditate more effectively. 21 effective meditation tips I wish I had known when I first began meditating—they would have helped me ease into my meditation practice in more fascinating and self-compassionate ways!

1. Begin Your Meditation Practice with No Preconceived Notions

Meditation is not a fast cure for all of life's difficulties. Meditation, like any other type of exercise, requires work and patience to receive the benefits.

Try not to walk into each meditation with preconceived notions about how you will feel or how much better you will become. Instead, look upon each meditation session as a chance to learn to know your mind better.

2. Don't be Concerned if Your Mind Wanders

When I initially began meditating, I gave up for months because I couldn't get my mind to stop wandering. I was irritated and upset with myself because I couldn't focus fully on my meditation.

It is, nevertheless, quite natural for your thoughts to roam. When I meditate and find my mind wandering, I just refocus on the meditation—there is no need for judgment or resentment.

If your mind wanders often, you should be proud of yourself for continuing with your meditation even when it wasn't easy and you were distracted!

3. Allow Thoughts to Come and Go

Try not to get attached to specific thoughts; instead, just allow them to enter and exit your mind. When I first began meditating, I would take hold of certain thoughts and analyze them (which just made me dwell on them even more!).

It's essential to remember that thoughts (and images) may arise for no apparent reason, and even if they're upsetting, we can recognize that they're simply thoughts and don't need to be over-analyzed. We also don't have to push thoughts away; they may come and go at their rate. Meanwhile, we can just be an observer.

4. If You Have Time, Perform Some Gentle Stretches or Yoga before You Meditate

I find that doing a few gentle yoga poses before I meditate helps me feel more comfortable during meditation. It also allows me to calm down and get into a nice mindset before I begin meditating!

5. Look After Your Breath

Breathing deeply and gently is widely recognized for calming the mind. But few people realize how much of a difference it makes to your mind whether you breathe through your right or left nostril. You will be able to focus considerably better in meditation if the flow of air via your left nostril is stronger.

It is simple to determine which nostril is prominent. Simply put your palm under your nose, exhale, and feel which nostril produces the strongest flow of air. If your right nostril is dominant, try laying on your right side with your head on your right arm for a few minutes to alter it. You should now sit for meditation as the left nostril becomes dominant. I know it seems strange, but it actually works. The Nose Knows, but for now, I recommend you take my word for it and give it a shot.

6. Minimize Distractions, But Don't Completely Ignore Them

You may choose to sit in a peaceful place with few distractions. For example, if a dog begins barking next door, practice attentive listening throughout your meditation by noticing the sound as it occurs and then returning your awareness to your meditation.

7. Begin with Brief Meditation Sessions and Progressively Increase Your Practice Time

If you're new to meditation, start gently and gradually increase your practice time. Begin with two-minute meditations. Once you're comfortable with that, extend your sessions to 5 minutes. Then go for 10 minutes. Continue to evolve until you achieve meditation sessions that are well-integrated into your life and enable you to reap the advantages of meditation.

8. Be Kind and Caring to Yourself

There will be days when meditation is easy and days when it is tough. When meditation becomes tough, be gentle and compassionate to yourself. Reward yourself for your efforts. Allow yourself a pause and self-soothe if necessary. Reassure yourself that difficult meditation sessions are normal, and keep in mind that things always change.

9. Keep a Mat on Hand for Comfort

It is preferable not to meditate on a bare floor. You have the option of using a soft yoga mat or a comfy low-height mattress. A soft cushion may also be used as a backrest for added comfort. If sitting on a mat is too tough for you, you may pick a chair with a suitable backrest. While meditating, make sure you're at ease.

10. Keep Your Phone Away during the Session

Because meditation time is your time, your phone calls and emails can wait. You are just concerned about yourself. Make sure you turn off your phone, put it on silent mode, or keep it in another room away from you. The entire point is to detach for this period of time so that you can reconnect with the world more effectively when you return!

11. Choose a Time of Day that is Ideal for You

When you set aside a specific time during the day to meditate, it is simpler to make the practice a habit, and you are more likely to do it every day.

For example, you might try combining meditation with an existing daily practice, such as writing before bed or drinking a cup of coffee in the morning.

If you find it difficult to remain aware during meditations before going to bed? Try meditating in the morning or late in the afternoon.

Do you feel hurried before work every day and the thought of meditating makes you feel even more overwhelmed? If so, seek to meditate when you come home at the end of the day.

Choose a time of day that works for you—don't feel obligated to do what someone else does if it doesn't work for you!

12. During Meditation, Try Not to Fidget or Move Too Much

It's normal to feel restless and desire to switch positions throughout your meditation. Feel free to re-adjust if it's too distracting or if you're in discomfort. However, don't let your position become a distraction in and of itself.

13. Avoid Meditating When You are Tired

There's a clear explanation for this: you'll probably fall asleep in the middle of the session.

However, there is another, less apparent explanation. It is considerably more difficult to stay aware when you are fatigued. Your mind may wander, your emotions may be more readily aroused, and the physical feelings of fatigue will cause you to fidget and/or sit improperly.

If you're very fatigued, avoid practicing until you've had some rest. When you're exhausted, the advantages of sleep will assist you more than any meditation.

14. Read Spiritually Encouraging Books

Your logical mind, which should remain calm during meditation, must also be satisfied. Set aside some time each day to read motivational books. Take a few minutes to read after meditation, when your mind is calm and clear. Reading spiritual books will encourage you to progress more in your meditation journey.

15. Instead of Just Once a Day, Meditate throughout the Day

Many individuals meditate once a day and then call it a day. Nothing is wrong with this. Some people's schedules simply do not allow for repeated meditations, while others are just not interested in doing it more than once.

However, performing many short meditations throughout the day may help you maintain your sense of peace, relaxation, and joy. It may also help you better control your emotions, think more clearly, and accomplish more.

You can meditate at random times. You may also schedule a meditation break at particular times, such as immediately after a work session or before beginning a major task. Alternatively, you may also set meditation reminders on your phone at certain times.

16. Have a Meditation Partner

It may be helpful to meditate with a buddy or a group. While we're rushing about trying to keep our commitments to everyone else, it may be difficult to keep our commitments to ourselves.

Meditation partners may provide you the support and encouragement you need to stay on track; your commitment to friends or a group is insurance that will help you maintain your practice.

Finding partners enables you to meet like-minded individuals and exchange experiences, all while keeping your practice exciting. Some individuals avoid group meditation because they are afraid of interruptions or feeling foolish, yet group meditations seem to provide a richer experience of practice for each person. It is a well-known phenomenon among meditators. They also offer a chance for people to share their experiences and evolve together. Spiritually, it is believed that group meditation is more effective for spiritual progress than meditating alone.

17. Don't Take Yourself Too Seriously!

Meditation may seem to be a serious practice at times, but it does not have to be. As you meditate, keep a gentle smile on your face. Allow yourself to struggle through a meditation session and grin about it.

18. Be Consistent, Even If You don't Feel Like

The strength of meditation comes from developing a habit and committing to it regularly.

Life is full of obligations, and our meditation practice may often be neglected in favor of getting more done than we "should" be doing. We may either skip it entirely or postpone it until later in the day.

Consistent practice aids in the achievement of higher outcomes. However, consistency entails more than simply meditating regularly. You should also attempt to meditate at the same time every day—early morning or just before bed are two great times that are tough to avoid. Another benefit of consistency is meditating in the same location every day. It's nice to jazz things up now and then, but your mind and body will get used to the soothing serenity and tranquility of meditation in the same spot and will respond as soon as you enter your space.

According to a 2018 research, meditation for 15-minutes per day improved positive well-being and decreased stress levels. According to the research, everyday meditation has the same impact on the body as taking a vacation.

So, although meditation may not seem like a vacation when you have to practice it every day, remember that sticking to a schedule is essential for experiencing these benefits.

19. Use Guided Meditation Apps or Enroll in a Class

If you find it challenging to maintain a regular meditation practice on your own, you may want to consider utilizing an app or class for additional accountability and assistance.

20. Know that There's No Such Thing as a Good or Bad Meditation

Don't seek for a certain experience while meditation, and avoid categorizing your meditations as "good" or "bad." Every meditation experience you have is right.

You may be attracted to a peaceful meditation with few thoughts; nevertheless, experiencing silence during meditation offers no more advantages than experiencing one in which your mind is busy or your body is restless. Each meditation session is unique and will provide you with precisely what you need at the moment.

You may discover that you spend more time in inner silence as time passes, but the best experience of meditation is felt every day while you go about your work.

Before each meditation:

• Bring an open mindset.

• Expectations must be set aside.

• Remind yourself gently of the real goal of meditation—to improve your life.

After meditation:

• Keep an eye out for small changes in your mind and body.

• Acknowledge yourself for doing meditation and seek self-care as a goal.

• Look for the benefits as they appear in your everyday life.

21. Introduce the Meditative Mentality into Daily Life

The goal of meditation is to increase your level of awareness so that your whole life may be changed. You don't have to turn out the lights and shut your eyes every time you feel the urge to meditate.

While a routine like this is beneficial, you can also incorporate that mindset into the more active portions of your day by practicing mindfulness. It is a meditative experience to do any activity being a witness and aware.

Simply by giving each moment of that activity your undivided attention, you may transform your everyday activities into a mindfulness exercise. Put yourself in the present moment without using it as a means to a goal.

Take in the entire range of your sensory experience when washing the dishes—the soothing water, the sound of the cracking bubbles, the shapes and colors of the items you're cleaning.

You may walk consciously; instead of being preoccupied with your thoughts, pay attention to each step, your breathing, and your surroundings. Maintain a high level of alertness and involvement in what you're doing—and if your attention wanders, gently bring it back to the present moment and what you're doing.

When you practice mindfulness in this manner, it changes your life. Meditation evolves into much more than a method as a result of mindful living. It becomes a way of life for many.

COMMON MEDITATION MYTHS

Meditation has been praised for its potential to improve mental health, alleviate chronic pain, decrease stress, grow spiritually, and foster a fresh awareness for the world around us.

Even with all of this interest, there are still myths about what this ancient practice can accomplish for human health and well-being.

The fact is that we often misinterpret meditation and end up concentrating on the wrong things. These misunderstandings regarding meditation make us believe that we cannot practice it. We get irritated, give up, and lose out on all the benefits it may provide.

If you've ever said to yourself, "I can't meditate," it's time to revisit the practice with a better knowledge of what meditation is all about. I hear a plethora of illogical ideas and misconceptions about meditation that adds to the problems that may prevent someone from continuing this vital practice.

Here are 37 meditation misconceptions to avoid if you want to reap the life-changing benefits of the practice:

Myth #1: Meditation is Dangerous and Should be Avoided at All Costs

Everything is risky. If you go across the street, you may be struck by a bus. When you meditate, you will almost certainly bring up a slew of unpleasant memories from your past. Suppressed information that has been buried for a long period may be frightening. Exploring it, on the other hand, is very rewarding.

No activity is completely risk-free but it doesn't imply we should cocoon ourselves in a protective cocoon. That is not life; rather, it is dying. Knowing roughly how much risk there is, where it is likely to be located, and how to deal with it when it occurs is the best approach to deal with it. That is the goal of this book. Meditation is the practice of increasing one's awareness. That is not hazardous in and of itself; on the contrary, heightened awareness is protection against danger.

Myth #2: Meditation Takes an Inordinate Amount of Time

According to studies, 10-minute meditation sessions may enhance concentration and memory, and even ultra-short meditation breaks can teach your brain to deal better with daily life. According to Michael Irwin, M.D., director of the UCLA Mindful Awareness Research Center, frequent practice may make you more tolerant, less obsessive about checking your phone, and less likely to wake up in the middle of the night. The effects pile within minutes, not hours.

Myth #3: Meditation is Difficult

This myth is based on the perception of meditation as an esoteric activity for saints, holy men, and spiritual adepts. Meditation is really simple and enjoyable to learn.

One reason meditation may seem tough is that we strive too hard to focus, we are too concerned with outcomes, or we are unsure whether we are doing it correctly. Being an observer during meditation, in my opinion, is the best way to guarantee that the process is pleasant and that you get the most out of your practice.

You can comprehend what you're going through, get over typical stumbling blocks, and develop a healthy daily practice over time.

Myth #4: You aren't Good at Meditating

Meditation may take a variety of forms, and there is no right or wrong way to do it. It's termed a meditation practice since we're working on improving our open monitoring and focused attention skills. There is no such thing as a 'good' meditator. The goal of meditation is not to silence your thoughts or to feel Zen-like and calm. It's a chance to rewire your brain for new habits and patterns by practicing a new way of reacting to thoughts, emotions, sensations, or distractions.

Myth #5: I Don't Have Enough Time to Meditate

If your calendar is jam-packed, remember that even a few minutes of meditation is better than none. There are busy, productive CEOs who have not missed a meditation session in the last 25 years, and if you make meditation a priority, you will do it. I urge you not to avoid meditation because it is late or you are tired.

In a strange twist of fate, when we meditate daily, we really have more time. When we meditate, we enter the timeless, spaceless realm of consciousness—the state of pure awareness that is the source of everything that appears in the cosmos. Our breathing and heart rate reduces, our blood pressure drops, and our body produces fewer stress hormones and other chemicals, which give us the subjective sensation of timelessness.

We are in a state of peaceful awareness during meditation, which is very pleasant for both the body and mind. People who stick to their meditation routine find that they may achieve more while doing less. Instead of working so hard to accomplish their objectives, they spend more and more time "in the flow"—in sync with the universal intelligence that orchestrates everything.

Myth #6: If You're Not Interested in Spiritual Matters, Meditation Isn't for You

People incorrectly label meditation as solely spiritual due to its connection with certain religious practices, but for many, it is just a method to achieve concentration and serenity by taking time to breathe and quiet the mind. Meditation enhances every aspect of well-being in the long run by assisting you in dealing with stress more effectively. Scientific data supports its advantages for migraines, inflammatory bowel disease, and heart disease, but it also aids in reducing the body-wide inflammation associated with many common health issues.

Myth #7: Meditation is a Form of Escapism

The actual goal of meditation is not to tune out and get away from it all, but to tune in and connect with your True Self—that everlasting part of yourself that exists beyond all of your life's ever-changing exterior circumstances.

In meditation, you descend beyond the mind's churning surface, which is usually loaded with repeated thoughts about the past and concerns about the future, into the still point of pure awareness. In this moment of transcendent consciousness, you let go of all the beliefs you've been telling yourself about who you are, what limits you, and where you fall short—and you come to see that your innermost Self is limitless and unbounded.

When you practice regularly, you clean the windows of perception and your clarity grows. While some individuals attempt to use meditation as a kind of escape—a method to avoid dealing with unresolved emotional problems—this approach contradicts all the wisdom teachings on meditation and mindfulness. In fact, several meditation methods have been created specially to detect, mobilize, and release accumulated emotional poison.

Myth #8: In Meditation, I'm Expected to Have Sublime Experiences

Some individuals are dissatisfied when they meditate and do not see visions, achieve a state of thoughtlessness, see colors, levitate, hear a choir of angels, or a glimpse of enlightenment. Although meditation may provide us with several great sensations, such as feelings of joy and oneness, they are not the goal of the practice.

The true gains of meditation are what occur throughout the rest of the day while we go about our everyday lives. We take a part of the calmness and silence of our practice with us when we leave our meditation session, enabling us to be more creative, compassionate, focused, and loving to ourselves and everyone we meet.

Myth #9: To Meditate, You Must Sit in a Certain Posture

While it's preferable to have a dedicated meditation space or at least one free of distractions, you may benefit from meditation's restorative effects nearly everywhere, even while walking, commuting, or bathing. Just be a witness to whatever you do or feel, that's it!

The Patanjali Yoga Sutras is a scientific study that delves into the nature of the mind in great depth. Maharishi Patanjali believes that it is more essential to feel comfortable and stable when meditating. It allows us to have a more in-depth experience. It is acceptable to sit cross-legged, on a chair, or on a sofa. You may even be laying on the floor, standing up, or even moving. You just want to be comfortable and not hunched over while bringing your attention back to the present moment when it wanders. Just remember to keep your spine upright as you begin your meditation. Relax your neck, shoulders, and head.

Myth #10: Some Individuals are Just Poor Meditators

This fallacy stems from the notion that you must be able to blank your mind, yet you do not. Thoughts are a necessary component of the process; therefore, you can't go wrong. Don't battle your thoughts! If you get distracted, recognize it and then bring your attention back by observing how you are feeling.

Myth #11: Meditation is Similar to Hypnosis

Meditation works as an antidote to hypnosis. In hypnosis, the subject is unaware of what is happening to him or her. Meditation entails being completely aware of each moment. Hypnosis causes the individual to experience the identical impressions that he is experiencing in his thoughts. Meditation frees a person from their perceptions. It clears and revitalizes our consciousness. Meditation increases metabolic activity whereas hypnosis decreases it.

"No one can hypnotize you if you practice pranayama and meditation every day," says Gurudev Sri Ravi Shankar.

Myth #12: There is Just One Right Way to Meditate

There are many forms to choose from, so explore to find one that produces the necessary soothing effects. You may have a live or recorded instructor lead you through visualizations or affirmations, or you can quietly or loudly repeat a word or phrase known as a mantra to locate your inner concentration. Other techniques include following your breath or including movements, such as tai chi and yoga. Whatever meditation technique you choose, the goal is the same—to be present.

Myth #13: My Mind is Too Occupied to Meditate

This is the most common misconception about meditation, and it is the most essential to comprehend. The human mind is constantly occupied since that is its job! It is believed that humans have between 20,000 and 50,000 thoughts each day, some of which are beneficial and many of which are not. To give background, some compare the synthesis of thoughts by the mind to the production of saliva by the salivary gland. Although it is not the most pleasant picture, it helps us realize that the flow of thoughts is constantly present. The solution is to be an observer of the mind, see your mind as a theatre screen in which various thoughts come and pass.

Myth #14: Receiving Any Benefits from Meditation Requires Years of Devoted Practice

The truth is that meditation has both immediate and long-term advantages. Benefits can be felt the first time you sit down to meditate and in the first few days of daily practice. Many scientific studies show that meditation has significant impacts on mind-body physiology after just a few weeks of practice.

For example, a landmark study led by Harvard University and Massachusetts General Hospital discovered that as little as 8 weeks of meditation not only reduced anxiety and increased feelings of calm, but it also resulted in growth in brain areas associated with memory, empathy, sense of self, and stress regulation. We often hear from novice meditators who can sleep peacefully for the first time in years after just a few days of regular meditation practice. Meditation has also been shown to help grow spiritually, increase attention, lower blood pressure, and boost immunological function.

Myth #15: It Provides Immediate Benefits

Many individuals start meditating in the hopes of seeing immediate benefits. While it is true that meditation provides calmness and some other benefits in a short time and may lead to deep experiences of inner peace, don't anticipate bigger effects right away. Meditation is not an easy practice. It takes time to become used to it and enjoy the real advantages of practice.

People who learn the discipline of meditation may need to practice for years before they achieve substantial results. Meditation is a skill that takes time to master. Although meditation may seem to be easy at first sight, the amount of mental and spiritual development needed to reach deeper levels of calmness is often enormous.

Meditation development requires practice and patience. Consider it as something you're crafting. Many basic and laborious procedures are involved in laying the foundation, all of which are critical to the structure's integrity. Skip one corner or omit a post, and the whole structure may collapse sooner or later. If you don't provide a solid foundation, your practice may crumble and you may have to leave it.

Taking the time to create a firm foundation by concentrating on the fundamentals guarantees that you are well-established before progressing to the next stage.

Myth #16: If I'm Meditating Right, I should be able to Minimize the Number of My Thoughts

The goal of meditation is not to cease thought since that would be impossible! In meditation, we are cultivating awareness of our inner terrain. We're meditating on our thoughts, emotions, and bodily experiences.

Every time we notice a thought, it is a moment of awareness! Instead of becoming judgmental of yourself for having a thought, remind yourself that the objective is to observe thoughts. And, rather than being irritated by your thoughts, use that energy towards fixing your attention. You may call it mindfulness on steroids if you can recognize when you're having a thought and prevent yourself from getting carried away by it.

Myth #17: Meditation is Focused Attention

Not at all! Meditation is a kind of de-concentration. Meditation improves concentration. While concentration takes effort, meditation is complete mental relaxation. When you meditate, you are letting go, and you are in a condition of profound relaxation, witnessing all experiences from a third-person standpoint. We can concentrate better when our minds are relaxed.

Myth #18: Meditation is Just for the Old

Meditation is a global practice that enriches the lives of individuals of all ages. At the young age of eight or nine, one may begin meditating. Meditation, like taking a shower, helps to keep the mind fresh and stress-free.

Myth #19: Meditation is the Control of One's Mind

This is perhaps the most common misconception about meditation, and it is the source of many people's dissatisfaction. Meditation is not about stopping our thoughts or attempting to clear our minds—both result in tension and increased mental chatter. We can't stop or control our thoughts, but we can choose how to see them.

Thoughts arrive to us on their own. We only notice them after they have arrived. Thoughts are similar to clouds in the sky. They appear and disappear on their own. Controlling your thoughts requires effort, and the secret to a calm mind is effortlessness.

You don't desire pleasant thoughts while meditation, and you're not afraid of negative ones either. You are a witness, and you transcend your thoughts to enter a quiet place deep inside.

Myth #20: Meditation is Ineffective If Your Mind Wanders

If you caught yourself having thoughts during meditation, that shows you were doing it correctly. Meditation is about improving our capacity to perceive different elements of our inner experience, not about altering it. The more we meditate, the better we get at avoiding being engrossed in our thoughts. This eventually makes us feel more in control and at ease, but the thoughts do not go away. In fact, when individuals tell me they had no thoughts during a meditation, I simply presume they didn't notice them," said Paul Greene, meditation teacher, psychologist, and head of New York City's Manhattan Center for Cognitive-Behavioral Therapy.

Myth #21: We have to Force Silence during Meditation

We can't do that; it'll just lead to more suffering. Although we cannot force silence on our minds, we may discover the silence that already exists in the space between our thoughts via mindfulness. This space between thoughts, often known as "the gap," is pure awareness, pure stillness, and pure serenity.

We meditate by focusing our awareness on everything, which enables our minds to relax into this quiet stream of awareness. When thoughts emerge, which is unavoidable, we do not need to criticize them or attempt to drive them away. Instead, we gradually restore our awareness. There are times in every meditation, even if they are just microseconds, when the mind dives into the gap and feels the refreshment of pure consciousness. You will spend more and more time in this state of expanded awareness and stillness as you meditate regularly.

Be assured that even if you feel like you've been meditating wrong, you'll still reap the advantages. You have not failed or wasted your time. You most likely believed you were your thoughts. Simply seeing that you are thought is a breakthrough because it starts to change your internal reference point from ego mind to witnessing awareness. You feel more at ease and open to new possibilities as you become less associated with your thoughts and beliefs.

Myth #22: Meditation is a Method of Avoiding Conflicts

That's not true! Meditation, on the other hand, enables you to confront difficulties with a smile. You develop the ability to manage problems nicely and productively. You gain the ability to accept things as they are and take deliberate action. You don't dwell on the past or fret about the future. Meditation helps to build inner strength and self-esteem. Even though difficulties occur in life, consistent meditation practice allows us to move forward confidently and quickly.

Myth #23: Meditation is Just for Saints and Sadhus

Of sure, most holy men meditate, but they don't meditate just because they're holy. They are holy persons because they meditate; meditation is how they arrived at this position. And they began pondering before being holy; else they would not be holy. This is a critical point.

A significant percentage of people seem to believe that before starting to meditate, one should be fully moral. It is an ineffective approach. As a requirement, morality requires a certain level of mental control. You can't follow any set of moral principles unless you have some self-control, and if your mind is constantly spinning like a fruit cylinder in a slot machine, self-control is extremely improbable.

Morality, mindfulness, and wisdom are three essential components of any meditation practice. As your practice progresses, these three variables become more intertwined. Because each one affects the others, you develop all three at the same time. When you know to fully comprehend a situation, compassion for all people involved is instinctive, and compassion implies that you naturally refrain from any thought, word, or action that may hurt yourself or others; thus, your actions become moral.

Myth #24: To Feel Bliss, You Must Meditate for Hours

You do not need to sit for hours to have a more in-depth experience. The link to that inner realm, your source, may happen in a split second. A 20-minute session of meditation twice a day will lead you inside. When you meditate daily, the quality of your meditation will improve. You will also begin to reap the real advantages of meditation.

Myth #25: For Max Effect, Meditate Only at Certain Times and in Specific Directions

Anytime is a wonderful time to meditate, and any direction is a good direction to meditate. The only thing to remember is that your stomach should not be full, otherwise you will fall asleep instead of meditating. However, meditating during dawn and sunset is a wonderful habit. It keeps you energized and relaxed throughout the day.

Myth #26: Meditation is Just a Form of Relaxation

The word 'just' is the major concern here. Relaxation is an important part of meditation, but it has a far higher objective. The statement is valid for some meditation methods. All meditation techniques emphasize mental focus, bringing the mind to rest on one object or one region of thought. If you do it firmly and completely enough, you will attain Jhana, which is a profound and pleasant relaxation. It is a condition of such extreme calmness that it resembles ecstasy, a kind of pleasure that is above and beyond anything that can be experienced in a regular state of awareness.

Most people come to a halt at this point. For them, Jhana is the objective, and once attained, the experience is simply repeated for the rest of their life. This is not the ultimate goal of meditation. The aim is mindfulness. Concentration and relaxation are thought to be essential companions to consciousness. They are necessary precursors, useful tools, and advantageous by-products. However, they are not the goal. The aim is to gain wisdom. Meditation is a deep practice that aims to purify and change your daily life.

Myth #27: Meditation will Weaken You

I've heard from many people that they believe meditation would weaken them and cause them to lose their edge. It's False! Meditation takes us out of the fight-or-flight reaction and into the present moment, where we may focus on responding rather than reacting. Meditation improves our concentration and boosts our performance.

Myth #28: Meditation is An Enigmatic Practice that Cannot Be Explained

Again, this is almost accurate, but not quite. Meditation addresses realms of awareness that go beyond intellectual thinking.

As a result, some sensations of meditation simply cannot be expressed in words. That is not to say that meditation cannot be comprehended. There are more profound methods to comprehend things than via the use of words.

You are aware of how to walk. You probably won't be able to explain the precise sequence in which your nerve fibers and muscles contract throughout that activity. But you already know how to do it. Meditation must be learned in the same way—by practicing it. It is not something that can be learned in abstract terms, nor is it something that can be examined. It's something you have to seek to comprehend.

Meditation is not a mindless technique that produces automatic and predictable outcomes; you never know what will come up during any given session. Every time, it's an inquiry, an experiment, and an experience. In fact, this is so true that when you experience predictability and sameness in your practice, you may interpret it as a sign that you've gone off course and are on the verge of stagnation. In meditation, it is crucial to see each second as if it is the first and only second in the universe.

Myth #29: The Goal of Meditation is to Become Psychic

No! The goal of meditation is to increase awareness. The goal is not to learn to read people's thoughts. The aim is not to levitate. The aim is to be free. There is a connection between psychic occurrences and meditation, but it is a complicated one. Such occurrences may or may not occur throughout the early stages of a meditator's career.

Some individuals may have intuitive understandings or recollections from previous incarnations, while others do not. In any event, these occurrences are not considered developed and dependable psychic talents, and therefore should not be given excess importance. Such occurrences are very hazardous for novice meditators since they are so tempting. They may be an ego trap, pulling you off course. Your best bet is to avoid focusing on these occurrences. It's OK if they come up. If they don't, that's great as well.

At some point in the meditator's career, he or she may engage in specific exercises to develop psychic abilities. However, this happens much later in the process. Only when the meditator has achieved a very deep level of Jhana would he or she be evolved enough to deal with such energies without fear of them overpowering him or her. The meditator will then cultivate them only for the sake of serving others. In most instances, this is only achieved after decades of effort. Don't be concerned. Simply focus on increasing your awareness. If voices or images appear, just acknowledge them and let them go. Do not get entangled.

Myth #30: By Meditating, You will Become a Sanyasi (A Monk or Recluse)

To meditate or advance on the spiritual path, you do not have to give up your material life. In fact, as you meditate, the quality of your pleasure increases. You may be happy and make others happy if you have a calm and tranquil mind.

Myth #31: A few Weeks of Meditation and All My Problems will be Solved

Sorry, but meditation is not a fast fix. You will see changes straight immediately, but the significant consequences will take years. That is just how the cosmos is structured. Nothing significant is accomplished in a single day.

Meditation is difficult in certain ways, requiring a lengthy period of discipline and sometimes a painful process of practice. Each session yields some effects, although they are often subtle. They happen deep inside the mind and only become apparent long later.

And if you're always searching for massive, immediate changes, you'll miss the subtle ones entirely. You will get disheartened, give up, and believe that such changes will never happen. Patience is essential. If you only learn one thing from meditation, make it patience. Patience is required for any significant transformation.

Myth #32: Meditation is An Excellent Way to Get High

In a nutshell, yes and no. Meditation may occasionally provide beautiful, pleasant emotions. However, they are not the goal, and they do not always occur. Furthermore, if you meditate with that goal in mind, they are less likely to occur than if you meditate just for the sake of enhanced awareness.

Bliss is the consequence of relaxation and relaxation results from tension release. Seeking bliss via meditation brings stress into the process, causing the whole sequence of events to unravel. It works the opposite way—you can only experience bliss if you don't pursue it. Meditation is not intended to provide euphoria. It will occur often, but it should be considered as a by-product.

Myth #33: Meditation is a Self-Indulgent Pastime

Meditation is indeed selfish if sleeping and physical activity are selfish. Meditation is a must-do for your mind and consciousness. It makes you more relaxed, less reactive, and more in control. This has a good impact on others around you and enables you to perform better.

Myth #34: Meditation is Primarily Aimed to Alleviate Pain, Stress, or Anxiety

In its original context—including and beyond Buddhism—the goal of meditation has been to explore life's meaning and purpose, as well as to connect with deeper existential consciousness. This fundamental element is often overlooked in the current time. The majority of research—but not all—focuses on the immediate health advantages of meditation rather than existential well-being.

The component of existential awareness in meditation practice is inextricably linked to the purpose and goals underlying meditation practice. So, if we want to really comprehend meditation, maybe we should put more emphasis on this crucial element. Learning more about this might also help ease some of the existing worries about using meditation methods outside of traditional settings to improve productivity and decrease stress.

Meditation can improve our health and well-being, yet its true power remains untapped and unexplored. So, one should do proper research on the real aim of meditation.

Myth #35: To Meditate, You Must Chant

While chanting may be used in many types of meditation, it is not mandatory for a good practice. Consider chanting or repeating an affirmation (such as "I am at peace") as a supplemental technique; actively repeating words or sounds may assist you in keeping wandering thoughts at bay. If you are more visual, looking at a picture or a candle flame may assist you in achieving a meditative state. You may also choose none of the above and simply be.

Myth #36: To Meditate, You Must Sit for Hours at a Time

Some practitioners can meditate for hours on end (this is standard practice at vipassana retreats, for example). While their dedication is commendable, if not enviable, such long periods of meditation are just not possible for most of us regularly. And the widespread belief that you must devote hours to meditation causes many prospective practitioners to believe they just don't have enough time.

Fortunately, meditation does not have to take up a lot of time. There are many methods to incorporate meditation into your everyday life, just as there are numerous types of meditation. Once you've decided on a meditation technique that works for you, you may choose how long you should practice it.

Perhaps 10 minutes each day is ideal for your schedule, or even less. You don't have to dive straight in either. Preparation for practice is equally essential, and it does not have to take a long period. You may start with anything as basic as 3-5 minutes of breathing exercises. While the duration of the meditation and its preparation does not need to be overly lengthy, you must commit. It is usually more beneficial to practice for a short period regularly than to practice for a larger period irregularly. Making your practice a habit can help you get the most out of it.

Myth #37: Meditation is a Religious Practice

Meditation may seem uncomfortably religious to many people. All of this discussion about spirituality and self-realization may be frightening, and it might even put people off from trying to meditate. While meditation may be spiritual and is included in many global religions, including Jainism, Buddhism, Hinduism, and even Christianity, you do not have to be religious or spiritual to practice it.

Meditation is not a religious practice. It is just a collection of techniques for reconnecting with your deepest self. It may also be a completely secular practice.

Although the terminology of meditation techniques may seem sacred or frightening at times (with words like "Nirvana," "Chakras," or "Kundalini"), it's essential to remember that it's simply language. The language is rich in history, and these terms are employed by certain practitioners to describe interior feelings or sensations. However, these are personal experiences that may or may not apply to you—and that's OK!

Meditation is a technique that leads us beyond the loud buzz of our minds and into a state of calmness and silence. It does not need any particular spiritual belief, and many individuals of many faiths practice meditation without contradiction with their existing religious views. Some meditators have no religious convictions, or they are atheists or agnostics. They meditate to find inner peace and to reap the many physical and mental health advantages of the practice, such as reduced blood pressure, stress reduction, and peaceful sleep.

Meditation allows us to improve the quality of our life. It allows us to appreciate everything we do in life more completely and joyfully, whether it's sports, caring for our children, or progressing in our careers.

I hope these insights into common meditation misconceptions may assist you in fine-tuning your practice. Take pleasure in the little stages as you evolve. And be assured, new levels of self-discovery will be unveiled organically at each step.

COMMON MEDITATION
FAQS

When most people first contemplate initiating a meditation practice, they typically have a few questions that they want to be answered—and after they start, they have a few more. Here are the answers to 26 frequently asked questions to help you get started on your journey.

1. Where did Meditation Originate?

Mediation's origins may be traced back to prehistoric times. Researchers believe that even ancient civilizations found altered states of consciousness and meditation states while gazing into the flames of their campfires. Meditation methods may be documented in Indian texts dating back 5,000 years. Meditation developed into many organized practices and forms over thousands of years, spreading throughout Asia, its continent of origin. It did not become popular in the West until the 1960s and 1970s. Since then, numerous varieties have spread across the world.

2. What Distinguishes Meditation from Relaxation, Thinking, Concentration, or Self-Hypnosis?

Meditation is distinct from these methods because it not only relaxes us but also fills us with peace, love, and optimism. It also progressively and profoundly changes a human being into a beautiful and joyful person. This occurs without much thinking, effort, or focus.

3. How to Bring Meditation to Daily Life Activities?

The most difficult aspect of acquiring a new skill or practice, such as meditation, is figuring out how to incorporate it into your daily routine. Most people have days when it is a struggle just to shower, let alone setting aside time to sit quietly and meditate.

Here's how to include meditation into your busy day—perhaps when you need it the most.

Mindfulness is the key! By incorporating mindfulness into your everyday life, you may get the advantages of meditation throughout the day. By being a witness to your bodily activities, you will be able to incorporate your meditation practice into your everyday tasks and attain long-term peace and awareness. For example, observe how your hand goes towards your mouth to feed the body; take notice of the smell, taste, and texture of the food; and observe how the food is chewed. These little practices may have far-reaching effects.

4. When is the Ideal Time to Meditate?

Although, the ideal time to meditate depends on our lifestyle, work, and the different activities we have to do each day, early in the morning, before sunrise, is generally the best time to meditate. At such a moment, one may sense the stillness inside as though it were a beautiful symphony with nature. It is particularly effective if the individual feels well rested after a decent, regular night's sleep. The evening is also a time of day when we may readily get into meditation. Just as we feel the urge to begin our daily routine pleasantly in the morning, after a long day at work, we want to unwind in the evening.

5. What Should I Wear While Meditating?

You may wear anything you want as long as it is comfortable for you. It's also a good idea to remove any uncomfortable shoes and relax any tight clothes, such as ties or belts if they're irritating you.

6. What's the Significance of Routine?

Daily meditation may improve your work performance! According to research, meditation increases your concentration and attention, as well as your capacity to multitask. Meditation helps us clear our thoughts and concentrate on the present moment—which increases productivity significantly. Additionally, the real rewards of meditation are seen when practiced daily.

7. Is There a Certain Way I Should Breathe?

Nope. When we meditate, we are not attempting to breathe in a certain manner. Allow your breathing to be natural.

8. How Long Should I Sustain My Meditation Sessions?

It is beneficial to allow ourselves the time we need to reflect and discover that wonderful stillness inside. To that aim, it is usually recommended that you meditate for at least 15 minutes. Because the entire length of the meditation may not have the same quality or depth, particularly if we have never tried meditating before, the aim should be 15 minutes of excellent meditation. Accepting and embracing the thoughts that may arise is strongly advised to reach a genuinely meditative state. Then the true meditation will occur and you will be able to enter stillness.

9. What Should I Do If I Feel Restless or Uncomfortable while Meditating?

If you feel restless or uncomfortable when meditating, it may be good to know that you are not alone. Everyone has moments of irritation or pain throughout their meditation (or even often). Meditation, in effect, works like a mirror, reflecting you back to yourself. That, believe it or not, is one of its merits. When you take a few minutes out of your hectic day to sit quietly, you may become aware of the anxious energy and frantic thoughts that have been bothering you.

As your meditation deepens, you may broaden your awareness to encompass your sensations, followed by your thoughts and emotions. At this point, you may start exploring, becoming friends with, and eventually accept your restlessness and discomfort. Though this process is not simple, it has far-reaching effects since it teaches you the resilience and peace of mind required to tolerate inevitable challenges in all aspects of your life.

10. What Should I Do If I Continue to Fall Asleep while Meditating?

Sleepiness, like restlessness, is a frequent impediment on the path of meditation. First, you may want to investigate the sleepiness. Where in your body do you feel it? Is it only cerebral dullness, or are you also physically tired? Perhaps you should take a sleep instead of meditating!

If you decide to continue, try opening your eyes wide and sitting up as straight as you can to reawaken your vitality. If you're still tired, try splashing cold water on your face or meditating while standing or walking. In any case, sleepiness does not have to keep you from meditating. After all, sleepy meditation is preferable to none at all.

11. What's the Significance of Keeping the Spine Straight?

The spine, being the origin of core energy channels known as Chakras and neurons, is very important in the meditation process. Holding a posture with a straight back in meditation opens you both energetically and spiritually. You cannot engage in "true" meditation if this is not present.

So, with each inhalation, raise your body and extend your spine. Feel the energy line that runs from the base of your spine to the crown of your head. Maintaining a straight spine can assist you in being aware.

12. How can I Know If I'm Meditating Right?

The wonderful thing about meditation is that you can't go wrong unless you don't practice it at all. (In fact, perfectionism is the root of most of your stress.) And the purpose of meditation is to decrease stress, not to increase it.

When it comes to recognizing whether your meditation is "working" or not, you're unlikely to see any blazing lights or unexpected bursts of energy. Instead, you may notice more subtle changes. Don't expect results, otherwise, your meditation may never come to a boil. Simply trust the process and let the changes take care of themselves.

13. Can I Meditate while Eating or Working on My PC?

Although you cannot practice formal meditation while engaging in everyday activities, you may practice doing things in a mindful way. During your daily times of silent meditation, you learn how to remain as present as possible in the face of a flurry of distracting thoughts, emotions, and sensations. When you go behind the wheel of your vehicle (your body) or sit down in front of your computer, you can use at least part of the same mindful, attentive presence to navigate rush-hour traffic or write a report.

You'll discover that you can do the activity with less effort and strain while also having more fun.

14. How Breath Rhythm Affects Our Emotions?

The way we breathe is inextricably connected to how we feel. We breathe slowly when we are peaceful, and rapidly when we are worried. When we relax our breathing, the levels of oxygen and carbon dioxide in our bodies are balanced, allowing our bodies to operate more effectively.

The amygdala's activity shows that rapid breathing rates may trigger emotions of anxiety, rage, or fear. Other studies have shown that while we are breathing rapidly, we are more sensitive to fear. Slowing our breath, on the other hand, may decrease fear and anxiety.

15. Do I Have to Abandon My Religious Views to Meditate?

Certainly not! The fundamental concepts and methods of meditation may apply to any spiritual or religious tradition or viewpoint. In fact, many individuals find that Eastern-inspired meditation techniques strengthen their connection to their own Western religion by complementing prayer and belief with some direct sense of God's love and presence.

Simply stopping in your hectic life, taking a few deep breaths, sitting quietly, and focusing your attention inside is what meditation entails. What you find is not Zen, Sufism, or Hinduism, but you, with all your beliefs, connections, and personality characteristics!

16. What Should I Do If My Family does not Support My Meditation Practice?

If your loved ones are overtly hostile, you may need to meditate on the sly or with a pre-existing group or class outside your house. However, if they are just stubborn or interrupt you at inconvenient times or demand your attention when you are about to become quiet, you should speak with them and explain your interest in meditation. Who knows? They may decide to join you and try meditation themselves one day.

17. What's the Right and Wrong Attitude for Meditation?

The Right Way: Meditating is a peaceful way of recognizing and observing whatever occurs, whether good or bad. Meditating entails carefully observing and waiting with awareness and comprehension. Meditation is NOT attempting to have an experience based on anything you have read or heard about.

The Wrong Way: The only way to go wrong is to get swept away by a thought or feeling. When you notice a thought or feeling, recognize it but let it go. Also, refrain from criticizing yourself for your mind wandering.

18. Is It True that Meditation may Improve My Health?

Yes, meditation may help you get healthier, both physically and mentally! Hundreds of researches on the health advantages of meditation have been published, and the findings consistently show that individuals who meditate frequently have better health than those who do not. Furthermore, meditation has been shown to relieve stress and depression.

19. Can I Meditate while Keeping My Eyes Open?

Closed-eye meditation has the benefit of assisting you in moving into deeper levels of meditation. Beginners, on the other hand, may discover that their minds wander more while their eyes are closed, or that they are more prone to fall asleep. Meditation with your eyes open allows your mind to be more present and attentive, which may make incorporating the meditation state into your everyday life simpler.

As a result, both are valid. Some traditions shut the eyelids during meditation (primarily Hindu-based practices); others keep the eyes half-open, with the focus resting at a location in front of you (usually in Buddhist and Chinese traditions).

20. What is the Best Meditation Method for Me?

There are many forms of meditation, some of which are very distinct from one another. Most of these methods are free to learn (through the internet or in a center).

It's a good idea to try all the ones you're interested in at first, but be sure to practice each one for at least a few days to get a true taste of it. Once you've discovered one that works well for you, you'll grow more by staying with it rather than bouncing around to other practices.

21. Is There a Kind of Meditation that is Superior to Others?

Yes, the one that suits you. All genuine types of meditation will provide a similar set of benefits and outcomes, such as increased mental concentration, stress reduction, increased willpower, spiritual growth, and so on.

22. What Should I Do If I Have Leg or Back Pain?

Even if you are attempting to remain completely still, it is OK to shift your body slightly if necessary. However, any physical discomfort will usually decrease with time as your body becomes used to sitting in that position for long periods. If you've been doing it for a long time and still have discomfort, try a new position, such as sitting on a chair or kneeling on a wooden meditation bench.

23. What is the Point of Meditation If It is So Boring?

It may be dull at first, but that will change. Keep going. Take things slowly at first. Meditation is about resting in oneself, about being the seer rather than being seen.

24. How Group Meditation is Better than Meditating Alone?

When people meditate together, they generate synergy. When a large group of individuals meditates together, those experiences are amplified, and the effects spread to the surrounding environment. Group meditation cultivates healing power that is much more powerful than meditating alone. Some studies show that when a group meditates together, there is a ripple effect of peace in the surrounding environment.

25. What If I am Unable to Feel Anything in My Body?

Many individuals are slightly detached from their direct bodily experience. Mindfulness of body and breath is a practice that requires work to identify sensations and be sensitive to the felt sense of what is going on within you. Consider if you have judgment about not experiencing anything in your body, and keep in mind that you are not alone. Also, have faith that embodied consciousness may be awakened.

Begin by scanning your body and noting where you experience neutral or somewhat pleasant feelings, such as the touch between your clothing and your skin, sensations in your hands or feet, coldness or warmth. Tensing and relaxing a bodily area may assist to make feelings more visible—for example, increasing blood flow makes it easier to sense tingling, pulsing, heat, and so on.

We often isolate ourselves from bodily sensations and emotions because they are intense, unfamiliar, or unpleasant. Instead, explore if you can get interested in the life of the body as it is. Allow yourself to befriend everything you encounter with a calm, kind, and welcoming attitude.

26. How Yoga and Pranayama Before Meditation Acts as a Catalyst?

Before meditation, yoga and pranayamas assist to calm and prepare the mind for meditation. Yoga began in India thousands of years ago, and in the current day and age, an alarming understanding of health and natural remedies among people has been noticed by yoga and pranayama, which has been proved an excellent technique for improving health and prevention and management of illnesses.

They are both ancient practices that aim to provide balance and health to the individual's physical, mental, emotional, and spiritual aspects. It has long been a widespread practice in India, and it is becoming more prevalent in Western culture. The term "Yoga" refers to the unification of our individual consciousness with the Universal Divine Consciousness in a superconscious condition known as Samadhi.

Their therapeutic potential is being studied as scientific study expands. Yoga and Pranayamas before meditation have been shown to decrease stress and anxiety, as well as enhance autonomic functioning by activating neurohormonal processes and suppressing sympathetic activity.

27. What's the Role of Gunas and Ayurveda on Meditation?

The food we consume has a significant impact on our state of mind.

Ayurveda, the ancient science of life, categorizes human body types and their Doshas or imbalances into 3 basic categories— Vata, Pitta, and Kapha. We also have Gunas (mental constitutions) known as Tamas, Rajas, and Sattva. Our personality, temperament, bodily structure, and dietary choices are all determined by a mixture of these Doshas and Gunas.

The underlying nature of the mind is to be calm, cheerful, and creative, or sattvic; yet, the proper balance of Rajas and Tamas assists us in fulfilling our everyday needs and activities. According to Ayurveda, there is a link between what we eat, how we behave, our health, and our mental makeup. We have the ability to react to and not react to situations by maintaining a healthy balance of Sattva, Rajas, and Tamas in our minds.

Tamasic foods diminish our awareness and cause us to become grumpy, pessimistic, and dull-witted. Alcohol, canned, processed, or deep-fried meals, very spicy dishes fall into this group. These meals provide no energy to us. We should strive to stay as far away from them as possible.

Rajasic foods are "activating." These meals stimulate activity, which means they raise agitation, anxiety, and impulsiveness. Coffee, spicy meals, soft beverages, sugar, red meat, certain fruits, onions, garlic, and eggs are examples of Rajasic foods. Rajasic meals are not always unpleasant, because they may encourage ambition and curiosity. However, we should limit our intake to prevent agitation, and they are not suitable for meditation.

Sattvic foods are those that are abundant in the life force and provide us with strength, energy, and joy. These nutrients make us more clever, creative, and expansive, as well as boost our feeling of tranquility. Fresh fruits and vegetables, whole grains, legumes, nuts, and seeds all fall within this group.

A REQUEST

Dear Reader,

As you near the conclusion of this book, I'd like to convey my heartfelt appreciation for sticking with me on this journey. I hope the pages you've read have inspired you, taught you insight, and sparked an interest in your spiritual journey.

Please consider posting a review on Amazon to share your opinions and experiences. By sharing your review, you not only contribute to common knowledge but also have a significant ripple effect of change and healing in the lives of many readers. If this is an ebook, here is a link that'll take you directly to the review section- Click Here

Thank you for your presence, for your support, and for your willingness to start on this transforming journey. May the knowledge contained within these pages continue to resonate deep in your heart and lead you towards well-being and spiritual growth.

Once again thanks for reading...

You can lend this book to your family, it's free of cost!!

You can also contact me for any queries: rohit@rohitsahu.net or on any of the following social media:

Facebook, Twitter, Instagram, Goodreads, Linkedin

Want to Hear from Me on Ayurveda and Spirituality? - https://rohitsahu.net/join-to-hear/

HERE'S YOUR FREE GIFT!!

If you're into Chakras and pursuing knowledge about Chakras Awakening and Vibrational Energy, this book will help you pave the way towards your spiritual growth. You can also join the mailing list to be the first to hear new release updates, improved recommendations, and bonus content.

Your 1st Book in the "Chakra Guidebook" series is FREE! This is packed with all the information, tips, and techniques that will make sure that you can effectively heal, balance, and open your Root Chakra.

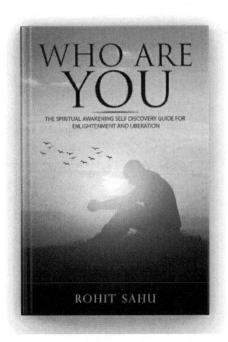

Have you ever thought after reaching your goal, why aren't you happy? It's because that is not what you need to be happy. This is not just another self-help book; this spiritual workbook will help you achieve liberation and be self-enlightened!

CLICK HERE to Claim the Books!!

BOOKS BY THIS AUTHOR

Ayurveda For Beginners (3 Book Series)

Ayurveda, which derives from ancient Vedic scriptures, is a 5,000-year-old medical ideology and philosophy based on the idea that we are all made up of different types of energy.

There are three Doshas in Ayurveda that describe the dominant state of mind/body: Vata, Pitta, and Kapha. While all three are present in everyone, Ayurveda suggests that we each have a dominant Dosha that is unwavering from birth, and ideally an equal (though often fluctuating) balance between the other two.

If Doshas are balanced, we are healthy; when they are unbalanced, we develop a disorder commonly expressed by skin problems, impaired nutrition, insomnia, irritability, and anxiety.

Vata, Pitta, and Kapha are all important to our biology in some way, so no one is greater than, or superior to, any other. Each has a very specific set of basic functions to perform in the body.

That said, when the Doshas are out of control, our wellbeing can be damaged. However, before we get into the particulars of each of the three Doshas, it is helpful to understand their basic nature and their wider function in the natural world.

Each of the Doshas has its own special strengths and weaknesses, and with a little awareness, you can do a lot to remain healthy and balanced. You can use this series to adjust your lifestyles and routines in a way that supports your constitution.

I've made a complete series of these three.

Just follow the books along, you'll reveal the easiest step-by-step routine to balance your Dosha by the end of it!

Ayurveda Cookbook For Beginners (3 Book Series)

All you need to know about Ayurvedic diet and cooking along with easy-to-follow recipes backed by the timeless wisdom of Indian heritage to balance your aggravated dosha...

I've made a complete cookbook series on all 3 doshas! You can use this series to adjust your lifestyles and routines in a way that supports your constitution.

With this "Ayurveda Cookbook For Beginners Series," I provide you the best dietary practices, recipes, and everything you need to balance and heal your doshas alongside enjoying the authentic Indian flavors.

This guide's Ayurvedic Cooking techniques tell what to eat and how to eat to help the healing process and assist the body in removing contaminants and maintaining equilibrium. It has a wealth of knowledge on healthy diet, proper food combinations, food quality, food timing, and cooking methods.

All the recipes in this cookbook are traditional, time-tested over decades, and are based on Ayurvedic principles. They can aid a yogi's yoga practice by keeping the mind calm and are thus ideal for all yoga practitioners. The beauty is that the recipes are not only sattvic in nature but are also tasty and have that authentic Indian taste!

Yoga For Beginners (10 Book Series)

Yoga origin can be traced back to more than 5,000 years ago, but some researchers believe that yoga may be up to 10,000 years old.

The word 'Yoga' first appeared in the oldest sacred texts, the Rig Veda, and is derived from the Sanskrit root "Yuj" which means to unite.

According to the Yoga Scriptures, the practice of yoga leads an individual to a union of consciousness with that of universal consciousness. It eventually leads to a great harmony between the human mind and body, man, and nature.

Yoga provides multiple health advantages, such as enhancing endurance, reducing depression, and improving overall wellness and fitness.

As yoga has grown into mainstream popularity, many styles and variations have emerged in wellness space. This centuries-old Eastern philosophy is now widely practiced and taught by people of all ages, sizes, and backgrounds.

There are 10 primary types of Yoga. So if you're trying to figure out which of the different types of Yoga is best for you, remember that there's no one right or wrong. You can ask yourself what's important to you in your Yoga practice: Are you searching for a sweaty, intense practice, or are you searching for a more meditative, gentler practice that looks more appealing?

Like you choose any sort of exercise, choose something you want to do.

Here's a complete series on all 10 types of yoga.

This guide can be used by beginners, advanced students, teachers, trainees, and teacher training programs. Covering the fundamentals of each pose in exact detail, including how to correct the most common mistakes, as well as changes to almost all body types, this yoga guides has left nothing to help you make daily breakthroughs.

Aromatherapy For Beginners: The Complete Guide To Essential Oils And Aromatherapy To Foster Health, Beauty, Healing, And Well-Being!!

Do you want to fill your home with calming essence and the pleasant smell of nature? Do you wish to get rid of stress and anxiety and relieve various physical and mental conditions? Are you looking to improve your overall physical, mental, emotional, and spiritual health? Do you wish to escalate your spiritual practices? If so, Aromatherapy is what you need...

Even though the word "Aromatherapy" was not coined until the late 1920s, this kind of therapy was found many centuries earlier. The history of the use of essential oils traces back to at least a few thousand years, although human beings have used plants, herbs, etc. for thousands of years. They have been used to improve a person's health or mood for over 6,000 years. Its roots may be traced back to ancient Egypt when fragrant compounds like frankincense and myrrh were utilized in religious and spiritual rituals.

Aromatherapy, often known as essential oil treatment, refers to a group of traditional, alternative, and complementary therapies that make use of essential oils and other aromatic plant components. It is a holistic therapeutic therapy that promotes health and well-being by using natural plant extracts. It employs the therapeutic use of fragrant essential oils to enhance the health of the body, mind, and soul.

Various techniques are used to extract essential or volatile oils from the plant's flowers, bark, stems, leaves, roots, fruits, and other components. It arose as a result of scientists deciphering the antibacterial and skin permeability characteristics of essential oils.

In the modern world, aromatherapy and essential oils have become increasingly popular, not only in the usage of aromatherapy massage and the purchase of pure essential oils but also in the extensive use of essential oils in the cosmetic, skincare, and pharmaceutical industries. Aromatherapy is considered both an art and a science. It provides a variety of medical and psychological advantages, depending on the essential oil or oil combination and manner of application employed.

With this book, I'll share with you every aspect of aromatherapy, as well as the finest techniques you may use to reap the physical, mental, emotional, and spiritual benefits.

This book brings light to the world of aromatherapy by offering a wealth of knowledge and practical guidance on how to get the most out of essential oils. It will offer the best option for living a joyful, natural, healthy, and homeopathic way of life. You will discover a variety of information on the best aromatherapy oils on these pages, including benefits, tips, applications, precautions, myths, and FAQs for using them safely and effectively.

You will discover the science of aromatherapy and how essential oils may totally change your well-being by using the methods mentioned. This book will help you use these potent plant extracts to start feeling better inside and out, no matter where you are on your aromatherapy self-care journey.

In this book, you'll discover:
✓What is Aromatherapy?
✓History and its Significance
✓Aromatherapy Benefits and Conditions it may Treat
✓What are Essential Oils?
✓How are Essential oils Made?
✓The Best Storage Procedure
✓How to Buy Quality Essential Oils?

✓The Best Way to Perform Aromatherapy
✓Activities to perform with Aromatherapy
✓Some Tips that'll Boost Your Progress
✓Essential Oils to Avoid
✓Safety and Precautions
✓Myths and FAQs

So, if you are interested in healing with minimum medication use, spending your time learning about essential oils is a good place to start. Just stick with me until the end to discover how this becomes your ultimate aromatherapy reference and the manifestation of your motives.

The Ayurvedic Dinacharya: Master Your Daily Routine As Per Ayurveda For A Healthy Life And Well-Being!!

Do you wish to synchronize your schedule with nature's rhythm? Do you wish to be disease-free for the rest of your life? Do you want to live a longer, better, and happier life? If yes, this book is going to be an important asset in your life…

Our generation is usually always going through a tough phase. Late nights at work, early meetings, and hectic social life are just a few things that add to our everyday stress. But the main cause for your distress is the lack of a regular schedule. Our forefathers never had to worry about stress since they maintained a disciplined Dinacharya that they followed faithfully. This helps keep the doshas in balance, controls the body's biological cycle, promotes discipline and happiness, and reduces stress.

A lack of routine can also cause many lifestyle disorders such as obesity, hypertension and stroke, diabetes, coronary heart disease, dyslipidemia, cancer, arthritis, anxiety, insomnia, constipation, indigestion, hyperacidity, gastric ulcer, and early manifestations of aging like greying of hair, wrinkles, depletion of energy levels, etc. Simple adjustments in one's lifestyle may prevent these numerous health risks and more.

Dinacharya is formed from two words—'Dina,' which means day, and 'Acharya,' which means activity. By incorporating Dinacharya's basic self-care practices into your life, you will be armed with the skills you need to foster balance, joy, and overall long-term health. It teaches people how to live a better, happier, and longer life while avoiding any illnesses. So irrespective of your body type, age, gender, or health condition, you should opt for a healthy lifestyle.

A daily routine is essential for bringing about a dramatic transformation in the body, mind, and consciousness. Routine aids in the establishment of equilibrium in one's constitution. It also helps with digestion, absorption, and assimilation, as well as generating self-esteem, discipline, tranquility, happiness, and longevity.

With this book, I'll show you how to align yourself with nature's rhythm every day so you may remain healthy and happy for the rest of your life. You will overcome all kinds of mental and physical illnesses in your life. The best part is that these suggestions are centered on Ayurvedic principles and are easy to implement.

This book covers:
✓What is Dinacharya?
✓Importance of Dinacharya
✓Dinacharya Benefits
✓Daily Cycles and Dinacharya
✓The Morning Dinacharya
✓The Afternoon and Sundown Dinacharya
✓The Evening and Night Dinacharya
✓How to Implement Dinacharya into Your Life?

✓Tips to Boost Your Progress
✓Beginners Dinacharya Mistakes

This book is perfect for anybody seeking simple, all-encompassing methods to live a more genuine and balanced life. You'll discover techniques and ideas to help you stay calm, balanced, and joyful.

Shadow Work For Beginners: A Short And Powerful Guide To Make Peace With Your Hidden Dark Side That Drive You And Illuminate The Hidden Power Of Your True Self For Freedom And Lasting Happiness

Do you want to recognize and heal the shadow patterns and wounds of your inner child? Do you wish to get rooted in your soul for wholeness? Do you want to influence your programs and beliefs to attain eternal bliss? Do you want to know where you are on the ladder of consciousness, and how to move up? Do you want to learn how to forgive, let go, and have compassion for yourself and others? Do you want to alter and strengthen your mindset to maximize every aspect of your life? If so, this guide is just what you need.

For many, the word "shadow work" conjures up all sorts of negative and dark ideas. Because of the beliefs we have of the term shadow, it is tempting to believe that shadow work is a morbid spiritual practice or that it is an internal work that includes the more destructive or evil facets of our personalities. But that's not the case. In fact, shadow work is vital to your spiritual growth. When you go through a spiritual awakening, there comes a point where "shadow work" becomes necessary. So, what exactly is the 'Human Shadow,' and what is 'Shadow Work?'

The definition of the shadow self is based on the idea that we figuratively bury certain bits of personality that we feel will not be embraced, approved, or cherished by others; thus, we hold them in the "shadows." In brief, our shadows are the versions of ourselves that we do not offer society.

It includes aspects of our personality that we find shameful, unacceptable, ugly. It may be anger, resentment, frustration, greed, hunger for strength, or the wounds of childhood—all those we hold secret. You might claim it's the dark side of yourself. And no matter what everyone suggests, they all have a dark side of their personalities.

Shadow Work is the practice of loving what is, and of freeing shame and judgment, so that we can be our true self in order to touch the very depths of our being, that is what Shadow Work means. You have to dwell on the actual problems rather than on past emotions. If you do so, you get to the problems that have you stressed out instantly and easily. And to be at peace, we need to get in touch with our darker side, rather than suppressing it.

Whether you have struggled with wealth, weight, love, or something else, after dissolving the shadows within, you will find that your life is transforming in both tiny and drastic ways. You'll draw more optimistic people and better opportunities. Your life will be nicer, easier, and even more abundant.

The book covers the easiest practices and guided meditation to tap into the unconscious. It's going to help you explore certain aspects so that they will no longer control your emotions. Just imagine what it would be if you could see challenges as exciting obstacles rather than experiencing crippling anxiety.

This book is going to be the Momentum you need to get to where you're trying to be. You'll go deeper into your thoughts, the beliefs that hold you back disappear, and you get a head start on your healing journey.

In this guide, you'll discover:

✓What is the Human Shadow?
✓Characteristics of Shadow
✓Do We All Have a Shadow Self?
✓How is The Shadow Born?
✓What is the Golden Shadow?
✓The Mistake We All Make
✓What is Shadow Work?
✓Benefits of Shadow Work
✓Tips on Practicing Shadow Work
✓Shadow Work Stages
✓Shadow Work Techniques and Practices
✓Shadow Work Mindfulness
✓Shadow Work FAQs

Covering every bit of Shadow Work, this guide will subtly reveal the root of your fear, discomfort, and suffering, showing you that when you allow certain pieces of yourself to awaken and be, you will eventually begin to recover, transcend your limits, and open yourself to the light and beauty of your true existence.

Spiritual Empath: The Ultimate Guide To Awake Your Maximum Capacity And Have That Power, Compassion, And Wisdom Contained In Your Soul

Do you keep attracting toxic individuals and set a poor barrier? Do you get consumed by negative emotions and feel like you can't deal with it? Do you want to heal yourself and seek inner peace and spiritual growth? If so, this book is going to open the doors for you!!

Empaths have too much to contribute as healers, creators, friends, lovers, and innovators at work. Yet extremely compassionate and empathic people sometimes give too much at the cost of their own well-being-and end up consuming the stress of others. Why?

These questions and more will be addressed in this book. You'll find the answers you're searching for to learn the facts on whether you're an empath, how it can work on a biological level, what to do to help you succeed as an empath, and how to shield yourself from other people's thoughts, feelings, and responses so that you don't absorb them.

There is a lot of things going in the life of empaths, and they are here to add more happiness and peace to the world. Empaths are known for their willingness to listen, sensitivity, empathy, and the capacity to be in the shoes of others. You may be that individual, or you might know that individual in your life, but either way, knowing the true cause of being an empath and why they are different from others will help you improve to lead a healthy, free, and beautiful life full of empathy.

This book includes the following, and much more:

✓What is an Empath?
✓Are You an Empath?
✓Is Being an Empath a Gift or Disorder
✓The List of Empath Superpowers
✓Ways to Turn Your Super Traits into Super Powers
✓The Secret Dark Side of Being an Empath
✓What It's Like Being an Intuitive/Psychic Empath
✓Signs You're the Most Powerful Empath (Heyoka)
✓Is Your Soul Exhausted and Energy Depleted?
✓Tips To Become an Empath Warrior
✓Empath's Survival Guide/Tips to Stay Balanced as an Empath
✓Ways to Save Yourself from Narcissists
✓Best Practices to Deal with Anxiety
✓Why Self-Love/Self-Care is So Important
✓Empath Awakening Stages
✓Best Transmutation Techniques for Raising Your Energies and

Right now, you can opt to proceed on a profound healing path and find strength in the deep pockets of your soul. Or you might want to put off the re-discovery of your inner voice and intuition, feeling like you might never have had it; never really understood how your powerful empathic ability can be channeled for the greatest benefit of all, including your own highest gain.

Filled with lots of insight into the inner workings of Empath's mind, useful knowledge to help you make sense of your abilities, and keep negative individuals and energies out of your life. This book contains all you need to become a stronger, better version of yourself.

That's correct, with this book, you can move out of your usual role and begin a journey. You'll experience the emergence of the inner energies and become a spiritually awakened person.

Who Are You: The Spiritual Awakening Self Discovery Guide For Enlightenment And Liberation

Have you ever thought after reaching your goal, why aren't you happy? It's because that is not what you need to be happy.

The major problem today in this world is that everyone is searching for joy in materialistic objects like money, fame, respect, and whatever. But the fact is, the most successful personalities in the world which you admire so much are not happy at all! If that was the case, they won't ever get depressed or sad. Is that what the reality is? No, in fact, they're the one who takes depression therapies and drugs to be happy.

What are all the fundamental problems that we all face? There is a sense of lack that exists in all of us, a sense of loneliness, a sense of incompleteness, a sense of being restricted, a sense of fear, fear of death. So these fundamental problems can only be overcome through self-investigation; there's no other way around.

Being happy is a basic nature of human beings, just like the basic nature of fire is hot. But the error we make is we're searching for happiness outside, which is impossible to achieve. Say, you wanted something for a very long time; what happens after you achieve it? You'll be happy for a while, but then you'll need something else to be happy, you'll then run after some other goal; it's an endless cycle!

The good thing is, there's a way to be happy at every moment, but to make it happen you must understand in a peaceful state of mind "Who Are You?"
You'll have to self-enquire! This book is based on one of the most popular Indian Scripture "Ashtavakra Geeta" that reveals the ultimate truth of mankind. It will open the doors for you on how we can achieve self-knowledge and be fearless. All your fears and doubts will come to an end; not temporarily, but forever. All internal conflicts will fall to zero, and psychological pain will cease to exist.

This is not just another self-help book; this spiritual workbook will help you achieve liberation and be self-enlightened!

Reading this book:
✓You'll attain everlasting peace
✓You'll understand the real meaning of spiritual awakening
✓You'll understand spirituality over religion
✓You'll get the answer to 'Who Are You?'
✓You'll be fearless
✓You'll be free from bondage and be able to achieve liberation
✓You'll get the key to everlasting happiness and joy
✓You'll grasp the real essence of spirituality and the awakening

self
- ✓You'll get to know about spirituality for the skeptic
- ✓You'll discover your higher self
- ✓You'll be able to experience the joy of self-realization
- ✓You'll find what spiritual enlightenment means in Buddhism
- ✓You'll know how to achieve or reach spiritual enlightenment
- ✓You'll know what happens after spiritual enlightenment
- ✓You'll get the answer to why you should have spiritual awakening

And this is a book not just for adults but also for kids and teens.

Chakras For Beginners: A Guide To Understanding 7 Chakras Of The Body: Nourish, Heal, And Fuel The Chakras For Higher Consciousness And Awakening! (Available For Free!!)

Chakras are the circular vortexes of energy that are placed in seven different points on the spinal column, and all the seven chakras are connected to the various organs and glands within the body. These chakras are responsible for disturbing the life energy, which is also known as Qi or Praana.

Chakras have more than one dimension to them. One dimension is their physical existence, but they also have a spiritual dimension. Whenever a chakra is disrupted or blocked, the life energy also gets blocked, leading to the onset of mental and health ailments. When the harmonious balance of the seven chakras is disrupted or damaged, it can cause several problems in our lives, including our physical health, emotional health, and our mental state of mind. If all our chakras are balanced and in harmony, our body will function in an optimum way; If unbalanced, our energies will be like in a small river where the water will flow irregularly and noisily. By balancing our chakras, the water/our energies will flow more freely throughout our bodies and thus the risk of imbalances and consequent illnesses will be reduced to a minimum.

In this book, I'm going to give you an excellent resource you can use to amplify the work you do with your chakras.

In this book you'll learn:

✓The Number of Chakras in Our Body (Not 7)
✓The Location of Chakras
✓Meaning Related to Each Chakra
✓Color Psychology
✓How to Balance the Chakras
✓Characteristics/Impacts of Each Chakra When Balanced and Imbalanced
✓Aspects of Nature
✓Qualities
✓Gemstones to Support Each Chakra

Step-By-Step Beginners Instant Pot Cookbook (Vegan): 100+ Easy, Delicious Yet Extremely Healthy Instant Pot Recipes Backed By Ayurveda Which Anyone Can Make In Less Than 30 Minutes

Who said healthy foods can't be tasty, I am a health-conscious person and love to eat healthy food, as well as tasty food.

"You Don't Have to Cook Fancy or Complicated Masterpieces. Just Tasty Food From Simple Healthy Ingredients."

Well, you don't have to struggle anymore with the taste. Here in this cookbook, you'll find 100+ easy yet extremely delicious instant pot recipes. keeping in mind the health factor, all these recipes are backed by Ayurveda, so yes, all are highly nutritious as well.

If you follow Ayurveda you know why we shouldn't eat meat or non-veg, so finally here is a Complete Vegan Instant Pot Cookbook. Plus, these do not require ingredients that'll hurt your budget, nearly all the ingredients are readily available in your home.

Every recipe is properly portioned and will be ready in 30 minutes or less. These quick and simple recipes will get your meal ready on the table in no time.

In this Instant Pot Cookbook you will find:

✓ Insider's Knowledge on How to Make the Most Out of Your Instant Pot
✓ Common FAQs and Other Must-Know Facts about Your Instant Pot
✓ Pro Tips to Get the Most out of Your Instant pot
✓ Things Not to Do with Your Instant Pot
✓ No Non-Veg, Complete Vegan Recipes
✓ How to Create a Variety of Healthy, Easy-to-Make, Delicious Recipes in the Easiest Way Possible

No matter if you're a solo eater, or if you cook for the whole family or friends, with these easy and healthy recipes, you can surprise your family, friends, and your loved ones.

This cookbook includes delicious recipes for:

✓Breakfast Meals
✓Stews and Chilies
✓Soups
✓Beans
✓Lunch/Brunch
✓Side Meals
✓Main Course Meals
✓Appetizers & Snacks

✓Light Dinner
✓Deserts
✓Bonus Recipes Including Salads, Drinks, and Some of the Most Popular Indian Dishes

Printed in Great Britain
by Amazon

32183360R00079